15TH EDITION

2025-26

ADRIAN RAFTERY

101 WAYS TO SAVE MONEY ON YOUR TAX LEGALLY!

THE ESSENTIAL GUIDE FOR ALL AUSTRALIAN TAXPAYERS

WILEY

First published in 2025 by John Wiley & Sons Australia, Ltd

© Adrian Raftery 2025

ISBN: 978-1-394-32863-5

A catalogue record for this book is available from the National Library of Australia

Registered Office
John Wiley & Sons Australia, Ltd. Level 4, 600 Bourke Street, Melbourne, VIC 3000, Australia

For details of our global editorial offices, customer services, and more information about Wiley products visit us at www.wiley.com.

Wiley also publishes its books in a variety of electronic formats and by print-on-demand. Some content that appears in standard print versions of this book may not be available in other formats.

Cover design by Wiley

Internal permissions: Tables 1.1, 1.2, 1.6, 1.7, 2.1, 2.2, 2.3, 2.4, 3.1, 4.2, 5.1, 6.1, 6.2, 6.4, 7.1, 8.2, 8.3, 8.4 © Australia Taxation Office for the Commonwealth of Australia; Tables 1.3, 1.4, 1.5 © Services Australia for the Commonwealth of Australia

Typeset in 11/14 pt Bembo Std by Straive, Chennai, India

Dedicated to my father in law George Davis who left an indelible mark on us all. He is sadly missed.

CONTENTS

PART I

YOU AND YOUR FAMILY   1

PART II

YOUR EMPLOYMENT   29

PART III

YOUR EDUCATION 65

PART IV

YOUR INVESTMENT PROPERTY 87

PART V

YOUR SHARES 119

PART VIII

MISCELLANEOUS   **241**

PART VI

YOUR SUPERANNUATION   153

PART VII

YOUR BUSINESS   197

ABOUT THE AUTHOR

Dr Adrian Raftery (PhD, MBA, B Bus, CTA, FCA, GAICD), aka Mr Taxman, is one of Australia's leading commentators on all matters relating to tax and finance. With regular appearances on TV and in the media, Adrian is one of Australia's leading tax and financial experts.

Part of Adrian's 'tax' appeal as a financial media commentator is due to his personable and approachable style. Just as importantly, Adrian's 35 years' experience as an award-winning accountant working with small and medium businesses, and as a personal tax expert, means he has the relevant knowledge and experience to give qualified advice.

Adrian is considered so good at what he does that he was one of the youngest Australian accountants to have advanced to Fellowship with the Institute of Chartered Accountants at the age of 33 and had an award-winning Sydney accountancy firm at just 25! Adrian is also one of the country's leading experts on the rapidly growing Australian superannuation industry with work from his PhD on self-managed superannuation funds published in top-ranked international academic journals. These factors and Adrian's ability to translate complicated tax, superannuation and finance jargon into understandable and workable solutions are probably why 'Mr Taxman' is frequently called upon for his viewpoints by the Australian media.

HOW TO USE THIS BOOK

This book is designed to be of benefit to 99.9 per cent of taxpayers. If you have an investment property, own a share portfolio, have money in superannuation, have a family, work as an employee or run your own business, there will be something in here for you.

While it is extremely unlikely that all 101 tips will be applicable to you, your family or your business, just feel comfortable knowing that one tip alone will be more than enough to pay for the investment you make in buying this book. This book has been written to take into account all phases of life, so if you find that only a few tips apply to you right now, don't worry because more tips will become relevant as you grow older. Make sure that you consult your own adviser to assess your own particular needs before implementing any of these tips.

If there is one constant with tax, it is change. That is why I update this book every year to take into account the latest federal budget changes and other Government measures each year. If you intend to use this book as a reference guide over a number of years, you should always check the latest tax legislation for the current figures and thresholds.

Remember that tax planning should be a year-round exercise, not merely one that's done in the last few weeks before 30 June. A lot of these strategies are just as useful on 1 July as they are on 30 June.

> ### ♀ TIP
> When you see this box throughout the book, it will provide you with a handy suggestion in relation to the particular money-saving strategy.

> ### ♠ TAX FACT
> When you see this box throughout the book, it will provide you with an interesting fact.

⚠ PITFALL

When you see this box throughout the book, it will outline a potential pitfall in relation to this money-saving strategy that you need to look out for.

🎁 BONUS RESOURCES

When you see this box throughout the book, it will provide you with a tool or a calculator available on my website www.mrtaxman.com.au to help explain or work out a strategy.

? FAQ

When you see this box throughout the book, it will provide you with an answer to a frequently asked question that I have received from readers of previous editions of this book.

📢 PROPOSED CHANGE

When you see this box throughout the book, it will outline a tax change which has been proposed by the government but has not been put through as legislation as at date of publication. Before making any decisions, ensure that you check the status of these proposed changes as there may be variations to the original proposal as it passes through both houses of parliament.

INTRODUCTION

Like for many people, writing a book — just one — was on my bucket list for years. So come 2010 I was really fortunate to get the opportunity to write the first ever edition of *101 Ways to Save Money on Your Tax – Legally!*

Back then I had three main objectives for the book. None of them were to make money (although my mates think that was the only reason!). First, I wanted to help maximise everyone's refunds by making you more aware of the different ways that are available to help you save money. I wanted to reduce the confusion around all the different types of government benefits and tax concessions that were available to you so that you started claiming more of what you were legally entitled to.

Second, through the setting of boundaries, I wanted to reduce the amount of fraudulent claims made so that we all pay a fairer share of tax. I am not sure what small part I played with achieving this objective but looking back at table 1.1 from the first edition it's hard to believe that the tax-free threshold was only $6000 whilst family companies paid an extra 5 per cent tax than what they will in 2025-26! Third, although this was never published, I didn't want my mates hassling me for tax tips at 2.45 am when we were out having a few beers. Needless to say as time rolls on, with age and families, this objective has also been achieved!

Whilst these objectives haven't changed over the past decade — and the structure of the book is still pretty much the same — I never thought in my wildest dreams I would be writing tax tips about cryptocurrency, non-fungible tokens, decentralised finance, the sharing economy, downsizer contributions and a crazy coronavirus that would cause a pandemic around the globe. Likewise, I never thought that tax incentives such as the education tax refund and medical expense rebates would be scrapped along with travel to visit your investment property. I guess tax changes is one of the few constants in life, along with death and taxes!

This book is split into various parts in line with some key areas surrounding your finances:

- you and your family
- your employment
- your education

- your investment property
- your shares
- your superannuation
- your business.

In each part I will share with you a number of tips and strategies that you can implement to save money on your taxes—legally!

You should leave no stone unturned in your quest to legally minimise your tax. While everyone should pay their fair share of tax, the late Kerry Packer summed it up best when he famously said 'don't tip them!'

Now I don't expect that every single tip will be applicable to every single person out there but I am confident that there will be at least one tip that will save you more than the cost of this book. Some tips will maximise your refund, others will minimise your tax, while others will simply save you money. Some may save you millions over a lifetime, others just a few dollars. But times are tough and every dollar counts.

Over the years I have dedicated this book to many amazing people who have had a huge impact on my life. My mum and dad (who have both passed away); my three kids (Hamish and Zoe on earth and Sophie in heaven); my wife Kylie; my university colleagues; the Irish cricket team; my neighbours; the Allies on Kokoda; community sport umpires and officials; the Bayside Bhoys; the frontline emergency services and healthcare workers and even the Commissioner of Taxation!

But I also dedicated two editions to two amazing families who helped us have Hamish and Zoe via surrogacy (the Donavans and the Merediths). Before we started the surrogacy process, I remember one of our tummy mummies telling us that she had a gift to bear children, but 'a gift is not a gift unless it is given'.

I feel the same way about this book. Ever since I started working as an accountant at the age of 18, I have had a gift (some would say a curse) for understanding tax. But as a gift should be given, I have decided to share some great tax tips with you for a small tax deductible fee (that is, the price of this very cheap book!).

Whatever you get out of this book, I hope it is positive and not too taxing! And this is my gift to you.

PART I

YOU AND YOUR FAMILY

From marriage and children right through to divorce, retirement and ultimately death, all families encounter many life-changing events. And in nearly all of these events, there are tax consequences along the way.

The Australian tax system offers a range of tax benefits including credits, refunds, offsets and bonuses to support families. Some people feel ambivalent about putting their hand out for government entitlements. But don't be shy in claiming your fair share. After all, the government doesn't get shy when it comes to taxing you!

✋ TAX FACT

Tax evasion and tax avoidance are illegal ways of reducing your tax payable. Tax planning and tax minimisation are legal ways of reducing your tax payable.

Part I looks at the tax concessions available to families, the special considerations you need to look out for, as well as some simple strategies to save tax within your family.

♀ TIP

You need a tax file number (TFN) to be eligible for any of these tax concessions, as do your spouse and your children if they have income, superannuation or investments.

1 MARRIAGE

Accountants are frequently asked two questions by couples who are just about to get married: 'Are there any tax implications once we tie the knot?' and 'Do we need to start doing joint tax returns?'

Your wedding day is a special day. So I'm perplexed as to why on earth the bride and groom are thinking about the ATO during such an exciting time in their lives!

You don't need to worry about tax in the lead-up to your nuptials. Unless you are involved in a business together, you don't have to lodge a combined tax return. Any share of joint investments, such as interest, dividends and rental properties, is still recorded separately in your respective tax returns.

> **♀ TIP**
>
> You don't have to lodge a combined tax return if you're married. Any joint income is recorded separately in your respective tax returns.

You do need to show on your return that you now have a spouse, and disclose his or her taxable income each year.

> **▲ PITFALL**
>
> The combined income of married couples is taken into account if you don't have private health insurance (an extra 1 per cent Medicare levy is charged if you earn over $202 000 combined, increasing to 1.5 per cent for couples earning more than $316 000) as well as when calculating Family Assistance Office benefits such as child care rebates and family tax benefits.

If you elect to change your name, you can notify the tax office:

* by phone on 13 28 61
* by post after completing the *Change of details of individuals form* (NAT 2817)
* or online via your myGov account at www.my.gov.au. Make sure it is linked to the ATO.

You will need either your Australian full birth certificate; your Australian marriage certificate; or your Australian change of name certificate.

According to the ATO, the definition of spouse has been extended so that both de facto relationships and registered relationships are now recognised. Your 'spouse' is another person (whether of the same sex or opposite sex) who:

- is in a relationship with you and is registered under a prescribed state or territory law
- although not legally married to you, lives with you on a genuine domestic basis in a relationship as a couple.

♦ TAX FACT

People living in same-sex relationships are treated in the same way as heterosexual couples for tax purposes. The ATO has outlined some of the tax concessions now open to same-sex couples, including:

- Medicare levy reduction or exemption
- Medicare levy surcharge
- dependant (invalid and carer) tax offset
- senior and pensioner tax offset
- spouse super contributions tax offset
- main residence exemption for capital gains tax.

It is not unusual to find a couple where each owns a main residence that was acquired before they met. However, spouses are only entitled to one main residence exemption for capital gains tax (CGT) purposes between them. If both members of a couple own a main residence they must do either of the following:

- select one residence for the exemption
- apportion the CGT exemption between the two residences.

Provided the homes meet the requirements for the main residence exemption, they will both be wholly exempt from CGT for the period prior to the couple being treated as spouses. However, from the time the couple became spouses, only one exemption is available, though this may be divided between the two dwellings.

✏ EXAMPLE

Mary bought a house in 1992. She lived in it right up to the day she married Matthew in 2006 and moved into his house, which he had purchased in 2000. As they elected to treat Matthew's house as their main residence, Mary will be subject to CGT on her house from 2006. She will not be liable for CGT on any capital growth in the 14 years prior to becoming Matthew's spouse.

2 INCOME SPLITTING

Income splitting is a legitimate tax-planning tool and one of the easiest strategies to implement. There are a few simple strategies for you to follow and they all mainly revolve around the marginal tax rates for yourself and your spouse, both now and in the future. The tax rates for individuals, not including the Medicare and other levies, are shown in table 1.1.

The goal is to try to level the income of couples so that they are paying tax at the same marginal rate. While income from personal exertion (such as your salary) cannot be transferred to the other partner, there is scope to have passive income from investments transferred if the assets are held in the lower-earning spouse's name.

TABLE 1.1: tax rates for individuals excluding levies (2025–26)

Taxable income	Tax on this income
0–$18200	Nil
$18201–$45000	16c for each $1 over $18200
$45001–$135000	$4288 plus 30c for each $1 over $45000
$135001–$190000	$31288 plus 37c for each $1 over $135000
$190001 and over	$51638 plus 45c for each $1 over $190000

Source: © Australian Taxation Office for the Commonwealth of Australia.

It amazes me how many smart business people are really dumb when it comes to reducing tax. Too often I see rich business people paying the highest tax rate (47 per cent including medicare levy) on interest or dividend income while their spouses don't fully use their $18 200 tax-free threshold. With the $2 million transfer balance cap on superannuation, there is an opportunity to split superannuation contributions between spouses such that each spouse maximises their respective $2 million thresholds before they retire.

♀ TIP

Ensure that all investments are in the name of the lower-earning spouse so that they can take advantage of the lower tax rates (particularly the first $18 200, which is tax-free) on any investment income derived. Likewise, have all passive deductions, such as charitable donations, in the higher-earning spouse's name as they may get a return of up to 47 per cent, depending on their income level.

The best tax outcome can be achieved with a low-income earner holding investment assets. They could earn up to $22 575 tax-free (see p. 15), receive a refund of all imputation credits and pay less tax on capital gains.

✒ EXAMPLE

If an investor on the top marginal tax rate of 47 per cent had a $100 000 capital gain on an asset held more than 12 months he/she would pay $23 500 in tax and Medicare levy. If an investor with no other income had a $100 000 capital gain he/she would pay $6538 — a saving of $16 962.

⚠ PITFALL

Any tax benefit derived by transferring an income-producing asset from one spouse to another may be lost if there is CGT to pay on assets originally acquired after 19 September 1985.

If you transfer an income-producing asset to your spouse you may need to find out the market value of the asset from a professional valuer. This is regardless of what you actually receive because the transaction is not independent nor is it at arm's length. In this situation either party could exercise influence or control over the other in connection with the transaction.

If you do not have a spouse, or you are both in the highest tax brackets, consider creating an investment company that is taxed at a flat rate of 30 per cent (reducing to 25 per cent if your company derives at least 20 per cent of its income from non-passive sources and has an annual turnover below the small company threshold of $50 million) for all income.

3 DEPENDANT (INVALID AND CARER) TAX OFFSET

The dependant (invalid and carer) tax offset (DICTO) is only available to taxpayers who maintain a dependant who is genuinely unable to work due to carer obligation or disability.

> **🖊 TAX FACT**

The DICTO has consolidated the following tax offsets:

- invalid spouse
- carer spouse
- housekeeper
- housekeeper (with child)
- child housekeeper
- child housekeeper (with child)
- invalid relative
- parent/parent-in-law.

The ATO may deem you eligible for the DICTO if the following applies:

- you contribute to the maintenance of your spouse, your parent (or your parent's spouse), your child (aged 16 or over) or siblings (aged 16 or over)
- your dependant was being paid either:
  - a disability support, a special needs disability support or an invalidity service pension
  - a carer allowance for a child or sibling aged 16 or over

- your adjusted taxable income as the primary income earner was $117194 or less
- your dependant's adjusted taxable income was less than $13482
- you and your dependant were Australian residents (not just visiting).

If you satisfy the above and your dependant's adjusted taxable income was $285 or less and you maintained him or her for the whole year, you can claim the maximum dependant (invalid and carer) tax offset of $3300.

⚠ PITFALL

The DICTO is reduced by $1 for every $4 that your dependant's adjusted taxable income exceeds $282.

♀ TIP

You may be able to receive more than one amount of DICTO if you contributed to the maintenance of more than one dependant during the year, including if you had different spouses during the year.

☝ TAX FACT

The ATO defines your 'adjusted taxable income' as the sum of the following amounts, less any child support that you have paid:

- taxable income
- adjusted fringe benefits
- tax-free pensions or benefits
- income from overseas not reported in your tax return
- reportable super contributions
- total net investment loss for both financial investments and rental properties.

4 CHILDREN

Any income that has been earned by your child's efforts, such as wages from an after-school job, is considered 'excepted income' and is taxed at the general adult tax rates regardless of whether your child is under 18. However, you should be cautious when putting investments in your child's name because minors do not enjoy the same tax-free thresholds as adults on this type of income, known as 'eligible income'. Table 1.2 sets out the tax rates that apply to minors' eligible income.

TABLE 1.2: tax on eligible income for minors (2025–26)

Taxable income	Tax on this income
$0–$416	Nil
$417–$1307	66c for each $1 over $416
$1307 and over	45% of total income

Source: © Australian Taxation Office for the Commonwealth of Australia.

⚠ PITFALL

Minors under the age of 18 are taxed at the highest marginal tax rate for 'eligible income' (such as interest, dividends and trust distributions) over $416 per annum.

If some of your child's income is excepted income and the rest is eligible income, they will pay ordinary rates on the excepted income and pay at the higher rate on the eligible income.

✎ EXAMPLE

Louie is 17 on 30 June. He earned $8780 from a part-time job. He also received $920 in interest from money he had saved over the years from gifts. Therefore, he has an excepted income of $8780 and is entitled to the tax-free threshold of $18200 for this income. He also has eligible income of $920 interest, which is taxed at the special higher rates.

A child is eligible from birth for a TFN from the ATO. If your child is under 16 (at the start of the calendar year) and does not supply their TFN to the bank or share registry, then 45 per cent tax will be withheld on interest earnings over a threshold of $420 as well as on all unfranked dividends. If your child is aged 16 and over, then the threshold is reduced to $120.

Children do not need to lodge a tax return if their assessable income is less than $416. However, if tax has been withheld from them by an investment body or employer, then they must lodge a return in order to get that money returned to them.

♀ TIP

If you have an adult child who has a job while going to university or TAFE then they may be able to claim a deduction for certain expenses if there is a sufficient connection between their course and their assessable income. Some expenses that they might be able to claim in this instance include:

- depreciation of assets (such as computers, desks and bookshelves) used for studying purposes
- journals and periodicals
- photocopying and printing costs
- stationery
- textbooks
- travel from work to place of study.

They wouldn't be entitled to a deduction for any tuition fees payable under HELP or any repayments of outstanding HELP debts.

Earnings from a child's investments must be declared by the person who rightfully owns and controls the investment, not the person whose name it is in, or whose name it is held in trust for. This is regardless of whether the money is spent on resources for the child.

If the funds in the account are made up of money received as birthday or Christmas presents, pocket money or savings from part-time earnings such as newspaper rounds, and these funds are not used by any person other than the child, then the interest earned is the child's income.

⚠ PITFALL

Children are not eligible for the low-income tax offset against unearned income, such as interest. The rebate can only be offset against excepted income.

5 PAYMENTS FOR NEW PARENTS

There are a few government payments available when becoming a mum or a dad.

Paid parental leave

Eligible working parents of children born or adopted may be entitled to the paid parental leave scheme to help them care for a new baby, dependent on when your child was born as outlined in table 1.3. If your child was born before 1 July 2023, the pay is for up to 18 weeks at the national minimum wage (currently $915.80 per week before tax) plus superannuation (from 1 July 2025) and is paid by either your employer or the government (where employers do not provide parental leave entitlements). For children born after 1 July 2023, the pay is increased by two additional weeks a year until it reaches a full 26 weeks for those that have children born after 1 July 2026. Table 1.3 also shows the minimum amount of days that are reserved for each partner, with the balance allowed to be divided between parents as they choose.

TABLE 1.3: paid parental leave

Child's date of birth	Maximum paid parental leave	Minimum reserved for each partner
Before July 2023	90 days	10 days
1 July 2023–30 June 2024	100 days	10 days
1 July 2024–30 June 2025	110 days	10 days
1 July 2025–30 June 2026	120 days	15 days
After 1 July 2026	130 days	20 days

Source: © Services Australia https://www.servicesaustralia.gov.au/changes-if-you-get-family-payments?context=64479#pplchanges

To be eligible you must have worked at least 330 hours across 10 of the 13 months prior to the birth of your child, but your annual salary must also be less than $175 788 (with a $364 350 family income limit if you do not meet the individual income test from 1 July 2023). The work test has been extended so that mothers can count periods of paid parental leave they've taken for earlier births as 'work'.

> 👆 **TAX FACT**
>
> Paid parental leave is subject to income tax and may also affect other government benefits such as child support, health care cards and public housing. In contrast, the Newborn Upfront Payment and Supplement is not taxable and not considered income for family assistance or social security purposes. For more information on paid parental leave go to https://www.servicesaustralia.gov.au/parental-leave-pay.

> 👆 **TAX FACT**
>
> Parents are prevented from 'double-dipping' into parental leave, where they have simultaneous access to employer-funded benefits at the same level or more than the government scheme. If the employer-paid leave is less, then they will only receive the difference.

6 CHILD CARE

Ask the parents of any young child and they will tell you that their biggest expense is child care. If you have a child who is attending child care services approved by, or registered with, the government you may be eligible for the Child Care Subsidy (CCS). You can apply for the benefit at the Family Assistance Office. The amount you receive will depend on the type and amount of care that you use, your income, the reason you are using care and the number of children that you have in care.

As can be seen in table 1.4, families with combined adjusted taxable incomes under $83280 will receive a Child Care Subsidy rate of 90 per cent of the hourly cap depending on the type of child care you use (shown in table 1.5), reducing by 1 per cent for each $5000 of income earnt by your family with no subsidy for family incomes over \$533 280. There is no annual cap on the maximum amount of the subsidy that families can receive in a year.

TABLE 1.4: child care subsidy rates (2024–25)

Combined family income	Subsidy rate (up to hourly rate cap)
0–\$83 280	90%
\$83 280–\$533 279	0%–90% (reducing by 1% for every \$5000)
\$533 280 and over	0%

Source: Services Australia https://www.servicesaustralia.gov.au/your-income-can-affect-child-care-subsidy?context=41186

♀ TIP

Due to the complexity of the calculations associated with the CCS, it is recommended that you overstate your estimated income with Services Australia during the year. This will avoid the embarrassment of having to repay some (or all) of your CCS received at the end of each tax year should your actual income be higher than expected (for example due to extra hours/overtime, bonuses, pay increases or capital gains). You can vary your estimated income up to twice per year. Any excess will be refunded to you once your returns have been lodged. To assist, the government withholds 5 per cent of the CCS upfront during the year to reduce the likelihood of getting an overpayment.

TABLE 1.5: child care hourly rate caps (2024–25)

Type of child care	Hourly rate cap
Centre-based day care	\$14.29 per child
Family day care	\$13.24 per child
After hours school care	\$14.29 per child
In-home care	\$37.87 per family

Source: Services Australia https://www.servicesaustralia.gov.au/type-child-care-you-use-can-affect-child-care-subsidy?context=41186#hourlyrate

Given the complexity of the subsidy calculations that flow from tables 1.4 and 1.5 combined with fluctuating incomes, to reduce the risk of overpayment, Services Australia withholds 5 per cent of your child care subsidy upfront. When you submit your annual tax return, the Department will finalise the annual child care subsidy that was entitled to your family and pay any outstanding amount due to you.

According to Services Australia, you may be eligible to claim the Child Care Subsidy if you:

- had a child 13 or under and not attending secondary school
- passed the work/training/study test
- ensure that your children under seven either meet the Government's immunisation requirements or have an exemption
- used approved child care such as long day care, family day care, in-home care, outside school hours care, vacation care and/or some occasional care services.

Parents can claim up to 100 hours of CCS per child per fortnight dependent on passing a work/training/study test. Once eligible, the rebate is paid weekly or fortnightly by Services Australia based on child care attendance information it receives electronically from your service provider. Even if your child is absent from child care, the Child Care Subsidy can still be paid in some situations. You can receive payments for up to 42 absences per child each financial year, if you are charged for child care. These absent days can be taken for any reason with no evidence required.

It is important to conservatively estimate your family income for the purposes of the Child Care Subsidy, because if you overestimate it you may need to pay back some or all of what you received during the year (even allowing for the 5 per cent amounts previously withheld by Services Australia).

Under the *No Jab No Pay* legislation, if your children (up to the age of 19) do not meet the immunisation requirements then you will not be eligible for Child Care Subsidy. Your child must be fully immunised, on a catch-up schedule or have a valid exemption in order to receive these payments. Note that while conscientious objection is not considered an exemption category, children with verified medical exemptions by a General Practitioner such as medical contraindication, natural immunity or participation in a recognised vaccine study are allowed.

7 LOW-INCOME EARNERS

There are a few tax benefits available if you are a low-income earner, such as when you work part time.

Low-income tax offset

The low-income tax offset (LITO) is a tax rebate for individuals on lower incomes. In 2025–26, the LITO will provide a tax rebate of $700 for individuals who earn less than $37500. The offset is reduced by 5 cents for every dollar that your taxable income exceeds $37500 up to $45000. The offset is then reduced by 1.5 cents for every dollar that your taxable income exceeds $45000, before phasing out entirely at $66667.

To be eligible for LITO, you must be a resident for tax purposes and lodge a tax return. The ATO will automatically apply this offset to your assessment for you if you're entitled to it. Minors cannot use the LITO to reduce tax payable on their unearned income.

> ♀ **TIP**
>
> Low-income earners can effectively earn up to $22575 each year tax-free after the LITO of $700 is taken into account. So if you have a spouse who is not working, consider an income-splitting strategy to save as much as $10949 in tax.

Superannuation co-contribution

If your total superannuation balance is under $2 million and your total income is under the low-income threshold of $47488 and you contribute $1000 post-tax to your super fund, the government will match it by 50 per cent with a further $500. The super co-contribution gradually phases out to nil (by 3.333 cents per dollar) at the higher income threshold of $62488.

Superannuation spouse contribution tax offset

You are entitled to a rebate of up to $540 if you make contributions into your spouse's superannuation fund, if your spouse's assessable income and reportable fringe benefits are less than $40000.

The rebate is 18 per cent of the lesser of:

- $3000 reduced by $1 for every dollar that your spouse's assessable income and reportable fringe benefits exceed $37 000
- the total of the eligible spouse contribution.

> **👆 TAX FACT**
>
> The ATO outlines that tax offsets and tax deductions are not the same. Tax offsets are taken directly off your tax, while tax deductions are taken off your assessable income, which is used to calculate your tax. So each $1 of tax offset means you pay $1 less tax, regardless of your taxable income.

Low-income superannuation tax offset

The government will contribute up to $500 annually into the superannuation account of workers on adjusted taxable incomes of up to $37 000 to ensure that no tax is paid on superannuation guarantee contributions.

Low-income health care card

In order to receive a low-income health care card your weekly gross income over an eight week period needs to be under certain income limits depending on your family circumstances. If you are single with no children you can earn up to $786 per week (or $1343 for a couple with no children). This increases to $1343 if you have one dependent child ($1377 for couples) and a further $34 for each additional child. You do not need to pass an assets test.

8 SENIOR AND PENSIONER TAX OFFSET

Senior Australians or pensioners may be eligible for an offset that allows them to earn more income before they have to pay tax and the Medicare levy.

As we saw earlier, if you are under the pension age (currently 67 and increasing to 70 by 2035), you can earn an income of up to $22575 before any tax is payable (see p. 15).

The tax rules get even better when you reach age pension age (or service pension age), as you may be able to access more generous tax-free thresholds, known as the senior and pensioner tax offset (SAPTO). Table 1.6 shows the thresholds for the SAPTO.

TABLE 1.6: thresholds for senior and pensioner tax offset (SAPTO) (2024–25)

	Maximum offset	Shaded-out threshold (taxable income)*	Cut-out threshold (taxable income)
Single	$2230	$32279	$50119
Couple (each)	$1602	$28974**	$41790**
Couple (combined)	$3204	$57948	$83580
Couple (separated by illness)	$4080	$62558	$95198

* Maximum offset reduced by 12.5 cents for each $1 in excess of shaded-out threshold.
** A taxpayer's taxable income is taken to be half the couple's combined taxable income.
Source: © Australian Taxation Office for the Commonwealth of Australia.

> **♀ TIP**
>
> Senior Australians are not required to pay any income tax if their income is below $32279 for singles (or $28974 each for couples). But if senior Australians derive income from a share portfolio they are encouraged to lodge a tax return, as they will receive a nice refund from all of the excess franking credits attached to their dividends.

> **🖐 TAX FACT**
>
> If you're single, you can earn up to $32279 (and $28974 each for couples) in non-super income without paying a cent of tax because of the application of SAPTO and LITO. Any additional superannuation benefit that you receive from a taxed source is tax-free.

Senior Australians who are over Age Pension age but still participate in the workforce can keep more of their pension when they have earnings from working via the Work Bonus incentive. The Work Bonus allows an eligible pensioner to earn an extra $300 per fortnight from employment before it affects their pension rate. Single pensioners can effectively earn $512 per fortnight (being $300 from Work Bonus and the $212 income test free threshold) and still receive the maximum rate of pension.

Any unused part of the $300 fortnightly Work Bonus exemption amount can be accrued in a Work Bonus income bank, up to a maximum of $11800. The income bank amount is not time limited; if unused, it can carry forward into future years.

Senior Australians who are not eligible for a pension due to their income or assets, may still be eligible for a Commonwealth Seniors Health Card provided that they continue to reside in Australia and their adjusted taxable income is below:

- $99025 a year if you're single
- $158440 a year for couples
- $198050 a year for couples separated by illness, respite care or prison

9 OTHER GOVERNMENT BENEFITS

There are so many different types of government benefits these days that it is no wonder some families are confused, and aren't claiming everything that they should be entitled to. Most entitlements are means tested, which means the benefits you receive are reduced as your income increases.

If you're in doubt when estimating your annual income, it is always better to overestimate. It can be difficult to repay a debt to Centrelink if you have already spent the cash!

Family Tax Benefit Part A

This benefit helps with the cost of raising dependent children and dependent full-time students under the age of 18. The amount of the benefit is determined by your family income as well as the number and age of your dependants. It will only be paid up to the end of the calendar year that your teenager is completing school.

Family Tax Benefit Part B

Restricted to families where the primary earner has an adjusted taxable income under $117194 with at least one child under 13, this benefit provides extra assistance to families with one main income. The lower-earning parent can earn up to $6789 per annum before the benefit reduces. The Family Tax Benefit Part B fades out when the secondary earner receives more than $33653 income per annum if the youngest child is under 5 (reducing to $26207 if the youngest child is between 5 and 13).

Parenting payment

This payment provides financial help for people who are the primary carers of children. It is means tested on both your income and assets.

JobSeeker Payment

If you are unemployed, looking for work and aged between 22 and the Age Pension age (currently 67), or you are sick or injured and cannot perform your usual work then you may be eligible for the JobSeeker Payment from Services Australia. The maximum fortnightly payment varies depending on your family situation but ranges from $781.10 per fortnight for single jobseekers with no children to $1011.50 per fortnight for single principal carers.

There will be a waiting period of between 1 to 13 weeks depending on how much you have in liquid assets and you will not be eligible for the JobSeeker Payment if your other income or assets are over certain amounts.

Income test

Individuals may be entitled to the full JobSeeker Payment if your other income is less than $150 a fortnight and your partner earns less than $2578 per fortnight. It phases out once you reach an income cut-off point (from $1484.17 if single with no children to $2725.75 if single and you are the principal carer of a dependent child with no mutual obligation requirements.

Assets test

Single homeowners must have assets other than their home worth less than $314000, rising to $470000 for a home-owning couple. These thresholds increase by $252000 for non-homeowners ($566000 for singles and $722000 for couples).

Youth Allowance

The Youth Allowance is a government benefit paid to eligible students, apprentices or those looking for work aged 16 to 24. It is means tested based on both the young person's income and his or her parents' income. The allowance is assessable and must be included in your income tax return. Unfortunately, Youth Allowance recipients cannot claim a tax deduction for expenses incurred in relation to their studies.

National Disability Insurance Scheme

People with a permanent or significant intellectual, physical, sensory, cognitive and psychosocial disability and aged between 9 and 65 may be eligible to receive support via the National Disability Insurance Scheme (NDIS). If you have a child less than 9 years old who has a developmental delay or disability, the NDIS has partnered with early childhood partners across the nation to deliver the Early Childhood Early Intervention program to assist.

Transition to work

Transition to Work provides pre-employment help to eligible young job seekers who are aged between 15 and 24 years, and are not involved in study or work. Eligibility is only available if the young job seeker does not have a Year 12 (or equivalent) or Certificate III qualification.

Home equity access scheme

If you or your partner are of Age Pension age, you own real estate in Australia and you receive less than the maximum rate of the Age (or Disability Support or Widow B) Pension, then you can apply for a non-taxable loan if you need extra income or to help for a short time or an indefinite period. The loan is capped up to 1.5 times the maximum rate of pension, paid fortnightly. Alternatively, you can choose to get an upfront lump sum payment but this is capped at 50 per cent of your annual pension. A no negative equity guarantee applies to these types of loans.

⚠ PITFALL

The principal from the Home Equity Access Scheme is accruing interest at a rate (currently 3.95 per cent) which is higher than what some banks are lending at. Whilst we all know of the benefits of compound interest when saving, with no minimum repayment back to the government, there can be sizable detriment as interest is charged on interest over time.

⚠ PITFALL

Under the gifting rules, the maximum amount that you can gift to a friend or relative is $10000 in each financial year and $30000 in total over the previous five-year period. Any excess amounts are added back as part of your assets under the assets test.

Seniors card

Each state and territory has a free Seniors Card scheme which provides transport concessions and participating business discounts on a range of goods and services. To be eligible you must be a resident of the state, 60 years of age or older, and not working more than a set numbers of hours per week in paid employment (for example less than 20 hours in NSW and 35 hours in Victoria and Queensland). If you work more than the minimum hours you may still be entitled to a Senior Savers Card or a Seniors Business Discount Card which has restricted benefits.

Other benefits

The following additional benefits may also be available to families:

- energy supplement
- single income family supplement
- telephone allowance
- stillborn baby payment
- education entry payment
- carer adjustment payment
- assistance for isolated children scheme
- pharmaceutical benefits scheme
- rent assistance.

10 FAMILY BREAKDOWN

While we all want to have the perfect marriage and live happily ever after, the sad reality is that approximately two-fifths of marriages end in divorce in Australia.

The tax system has provisions in place to assist with easing the financial burden of separating families. These provisions apply to capital gains tax (CGT), superannuation and income from child-support and partner-support payments.

Transfer of assets

Normally, when you sell an asset that was acquired after 19 September 1985, you are liable for CGT. However, when you transfer assets to your spouse as a result of the breakdown of your relationship, it is classified as an 'automatic rollover' of those assets and you will not have to pay CGT at that time. Any subsequent disposal of the asset will trigger the CGT provisions, except for the family home, which is exempt.

♦ TAX FACT

There is no CGT if you transfer a property to your former spouse under a court order following the breakdown of your marriage.

This rollover ensures the spouse who gives the assets disregards a capital gain or capital loss that would otherwise arise, and the one who receives the asset (the transferee spouse) will make the capital gain or capital loss when they subsequently dispose of the asset.

> ### ⚠ PITFALL
>
> If you and your spouse divide your property under a private or informal agreement (not because of a court order, a binding financial agreement, an arbitral award or another agreement or award), marriage or relationship breakdown rollover does not apply.

Transfer of superannuation

The splitting of superannuation between divorcing partners is similarly treated as a rollover. As the funds are not being released as a payment, this rollover split does not need to wait until retirement.

Child support and spouse support payments

You do not need to include any child support or spouse support payments that you may receive in your taxable income, but they are part of your adjusted taxable income calculation for tax offset purposes. Similarly, there is no tax deduction available for child support or spouse support payments.

The ATO cooperates with the Child Support Agency to:

- supply information to the Child Support Agency for the purpose of calculating child support payments
- encourage lodgement of outstanding tax returns
- recoup child-support debt from tax returns.

Some may say that binding financial agreements defeat the purpose of marrying based on the values of love and trust, but seeking legal advice on setting up a binding financial agreement could be a good preventative measure against a bag egg. Love hurts, but divorce can be expensive. Make sure you consult a lawyer before drafting up any such agreement.

Leaving violence payment

The 2024–25 federal budget announced the Leaving Violence Payment program to support eligible victim-survivors with up to $5000 to leave a violent intimate partner relationship. This includes up to $1500 in cash and the remainder in goods, services and supports. In a pre-cursor Escaping Violence Payment trial program delivered by UnitingCare, the payment has only been available to Australian citizens or permanent residents aged 18 or older who are experiencing financial stress and the victim of intimate partner violence that has resulted in a changed living arrangement in the previous 12 weeks.

11 DEATH

Three things in life are certain—taxes, death … and taxes on death! Unlike other countries, there is no gift or inheritance tax in Australia. But don't be fooled because certain transactions that occur as a consequence of a person's death are taxed.

Date of death return

Executors of deceased estates are required to finalise the tax affairs of the deceased person, including any outstanding tax returns.

The final personal tax return of the deceased person with their personal TFN is known as the 'date of death return' and covers the period from the previous 1 July to the date of death. It should include all assessable income derived by the deceased person and all the tax-deductible expenses incurred up to the date of death.

The general individual tax rates, with the full tax-free threshold, apply to the final tax return as well as the Medicare levy and Medicare levy surcharge. Any compulsory Higher Education Loan Program (HELP) or Student Financial Supplement Scheme (SFSS) repayments are also included, but the remaining accumulated HELP debt is cancelled.

> **♀TIP**
>
> Ordinary losses as well as capital losses will lapse at the time of death and cannot be carried forward into the deceased estate. If possible, try to use these capital losses prior to death by selling any assets that have appreciated in value.

Deceased estate returns

Income derived after the date of death, and any deductible expenses incurred after the date of death, are included in the deceased estate's trust return. Tax returns will need to be lodged in future years until the estate is fully administered and no longer deriving income.

For the first three tax returns, deceased estate income—to which no beneficiary is presently entitled—is taxed at the general individual rates, with the benefit of the full tax-free threshold. No Medicare levy is payable. In the fourth and subsequent years, the concessional period is not extended and special progressive trust tax rates will then apply, as set out in table 1.7.

TABLE 1.7: deceased estate tax rates (2025–26)

Deceased estate taxable income (no present entitlement)	Tax rates
$0–$416	Nil
$417–$610	50% of the excess over $416
$611–$45 000	$97.76 + 16% of the excess over $610
$45 001–$135 000	$7200 + 30% of the excess over $45 000
$135 001–$190 000	$34 200 + 37% of the excess over $135 000
$190 001 and over	$54 550 + 45% of the excess over $190 000

Source: © Australian Taxation Office for the Commonwealth of Australia.

A new tax file number is required to lodge a deceased estate's tax return.

Beneficiaries

A beneficiary is a person who receives all or part of the deceased estate. There may be some tax obligations for beneficiaries, depending on the nature of any distribution they may receive. If the trust distribution consists of:

- *Corpus.* There is no tax payable.
- *Income.* Tax is payable at the beneficiary's marginal tax rate.
- *Assets.* There may be capital gains tax on subsequent disposal; see p. 106 and p. 132.

⚠ PITFALL

Funeral expenses are not tax-deductible.

12 FAMILY TRUSTS

Trusts are an excellent vehicle for managing and preserving your family's wealth. They provide a great deal of flexibility in sharing the tax burden as income and capital can be distributed among beneficiaries in the most tax–effective manner. Beneficiaries generally have no legal entitlement or interest in the trust's assets until the date stated in the trust deed (for example, Billy is only entitled to the assets upon reaching age 30).

♀ TIP

If you are worried about certain family members 'blowing' all of the assets that you worked hard accumulating over the years, the creation of a trust will give you a bit more peace of mind.

Trusts are ideal for those beneficiaries who are hopeless with money, suffer from drug addiction, have long-term health problems or are likely to experience a relationship breakdown in the future. Essentially, family assets can be protected from 'creditors and predators'.

The two main types of trusts used by families are:

- *Discretionary trusts.* These are often set up either to hold property and investments on behalf of family members or to operate a business.
- *Testamentary trusts.* These are created via a clause in the 'testament' (or will) of an individual, but don't get established until after the individual dies.

A testamentary trust is an indirect way of managing your family's wealth after your death. While you obviously won't be around to oversee the management of the trust itself, you will have some comfort knowing that your loved ones will be looked after financially and not savaged by the ATO.

🔖 TAX FACT

There are substantial tax advantages relating to testamentary trusts, including distributions to minors being taxed at the more favourable adult rates.

⚠ PITFALL

The cost of establishing and maintaining a trust can be high and may outweigh any benefits in having a trust structure, especially when the assets involved are not worth much.

The trustee is the legal owner of the trust property, and is responsible for managing the trust fund on behalf of the beneficiaries. The trustee has a legal duty to obey the terms of the trust deed and to always act in the best interests of the beneficiaries. A trust can operate for up to 80 years in Australia, though it is common to have a clause within the trust deed to allow the trustee the option of winding it up earlier if considered appropriate. Distributions must be documented by 30 June each year.

The ATO takes a dim view of trustees who have distributed net income 'on paper' to certain tax-advantaged beneficiaries but have not physically received any payments from the trust.

There are many benefits to using trusts to manage your wealth, including:

- *Asset protection*. Family assets may be protected from 'creditors and predators' in the event of bankruptcy or insolvency in certain situations.
- *Australia-wide*. A trust established under Australian law can operate effectively in every Australian state. If you have potential beneficiaries living overseas, it is recommended that you seek specialist advice before proceeding further as there are many tax implications to consider.
- *Flexibility*. Trust deeds are flexible in their operation and can cater for a wide variety of beneficiary classes and investments, and different types of income can be directed to different beneficiaries.
- *Little regulation*. Trusts do not have as many reporting requirements and obligations as company structures.
- *Tax minimisation*. Income can be directed to family members on lower tax rates but note to seek advice from a tax professional before you do.

If you place money in a term deposit, consider having it mature after 30 June so that any income is not assessable until the following financial year.

PART II
YOUR EMPLOYMENT

There have been a few noticeable changes in employment conditions in recent years. Employees seem to be working longer hours as employers seek greater productivity. Employees also seem to be bearing the greater brunt of expenses as employers have become more cost-driven and hence a lot less generous in reimbursing work–related expenses.

👆 TAX FACT

Of the 15.54 million people who lodged a tax return in 2021–22, 9.86 million claimed $24.718 billion in deductions for work-related expenses.

Fortunately, employees can claim for work–related expenses in their income tax return each year and get a refund at their marginal rate of tax.

👆 TAX FACT

If you work in one of the following occupations or industries, make sure you look at the relevant ATO publication on their webpage www.ato.gov.au/occupations on claiming specific work-related expenses in your tax return:

- adult industry workers
- agricultural workers
- airline employees (including pilots and flight crew)
- Australian Defence Force members
- building and construction workers and earthmoving plant operators
- bus and train drivers
- call-centre operators
- cleaners
- community workers
- doctor, specialist or other medical professionals
- education professionals
- engineers

▷

- factory workers
- firefighters
- fitness and sport industry employees
- gaming attendants
- hairdressers
- hospitality industry employees
- IT/business professionals
- lawyers
- meat workers
- media professionals
- mining site employees
- nurses, midwives and direct carers
- office workers
- paramedics
- performing artists
- police
- professional sportspeople
- real-estate employees
- recruitment consultants
- retail industry workers
- sales representatives and sales and marketing managers
- security guards
- shop assistants
- teachers
- tradespersons
- travel agents
- truck drivers.

Part II will look at tax deductions that you might be able to claim in relation to your employment income, who the ATO targets, and ways to improve your cash flow and tax situation.

👆 TAX FACT

You can claim the cost of rapid antigen tests (RATs) if it is a condition of work and your employer does not reimburse you for them. However, any RATs for schoolchildren would be considered to be private in nature and are not deductible.

13 CAR USAGE

Taxpayers who use their car in the course of earning assessable income may be entitled to claim deductions for some of the costs.

The ATO has outlined that you can claim the cost of using your car to travel:

- from your normal workplace to an alternative workplace — for example, a client's premises — while still on duty, and back to your normal workplace or directly home
- from your home to an alternative workplace for work purposes and then to your normal workplace or directly home.

> **♀ TIP**
>
> To help justify your claim for car travel, have client travel included as one of your requirements in your job description or contract of employment.

You cannot claim the cost of normal trips between home and work as the expense is private. You cannot claim it even if:

- you do minor tasks—such as picking up the mail on the way to work
- you have to travel between home and work more than once a day
- you are 'on call' and your employer contacts you at home to come in to work
- there is no public transport near where you work
- you work outside normal business hours—for example, shift work or overtime
- your home is a place of business and you travel directly to a place of employment.

You can claim the cost of trips between home and work where:

- you use your car because you have to carry bulky tools or equipment that you use for work and there is no secure place for you to leave them at work
- your home is a base of employment—you start your work at home and travel to a workplace to continue the work
- you are an itinerant worker with shifting places of employment.

The following three characteristics will assist you in determining if your work is itinerant:

- travel is a fundamental part of your work
- you have a web of workplaces in your regular employment with no fixed place of work
- you regularly work at more than one site each day before returning home.

I am a painter by trade and recently purchased a brand new ute. I work full time and carry my gear with me at all times. I want to know what I can claim, and if I have to keep a log book even though I use my vehicle 100 per cent for work.

Given that you have a ute (commercial vehicle greater than 1 tonne) and clearly carry paint gear all the time, there is no requirement to maintain a logbook as it would be considered 100 per cent work use. However, if you want to use the logbook method then you will need to keep all receipts throughout the year for expenses such as petrol, registration, insurance, servicing and repairs as well as any finance payments (lease or interest).

14 METHODS TO CLAIM CAR TRAVEL

There are only two specific methods available to individuals to calculate deductions for car expenses:

- cents per kilometre method
- logbook (12-week) method

♀ TIP

If you often use your car for work, the logbook method is probably your best option for calculating deductions.

If you use the logbook method, purchase a logbook from the newsagent, fill it out for a continuous 12-week period and keep records of all costs associated with the running of your car including petrol, registration, insurances, servicing, repairs, lease payments, batteries, tyres, and so on. The hard work is worth it as deductions can be in the thousands and you only need to do a new logbook every five years unless you change your job or car.

Under the logbook method, you can claim a portion of the running costs of the car, including depreciation and interest, based upon your work-related use percentage.

Under the cents per kilometre method, you must make a reasonable estimate of kilometres travelled, up to a maximum of 5000, and multiply this by a flat rate of 88 cents per kilometre regardless of engine capacity.

You need to satisfy the tax office that the travel was undertaken for income-producing purposes and that your claim is calculated on a reasonable basis. Do not guess!

George is a mechanic who is required to travel regularly to pick up spare parts from a supplier. In his tax return, he guesses that he travelled 3500 kilometres.

A check with George's employer reveals that the trip to the supplier is an 8-kilometre round-trip journey, made no more than three days per week and that George also had four weeks' holidays during the year.

George has not made a reasonable estimate and the claim should have been based on 1152 kilometres (three days × 8 km × 48 weeks). Based on a two-litre engine, the deduction that can be claimed is $1014 (1152 km × 88 cents).

👆 TAX FACT

Under the logbook method, you can claim fuel and oil costs on either your actual receipts or an estimate based on odometer readings from the start and the end of the year.

⚠️ PITFALL

If you purchase a car for more than $69674, the ATO will limit your deduction for depreciation to the first $69674. While I say all cars cost money, they cost even more if they are expensive luxury cars (as you don't even get a tax break on the excess that you are paying).

15 TRAVEL

If you incur travel expenses in the course of your work, or in travelling between one place of business and another, they are deductible — for example motor vehicle expenses, air, bus, train or taxi fares, and car rental costs. Accommodation and meals on business trips away from home may also be deductible.

⚠️ PITFALL

Passport fees and travel insurance are generally considered to be private in nature and are not deductible.

If you want to claim travel expenses, you need to keep a travel diary. This applies to work-related trips interstate or overseas of more than five days. It must detail dates, places, times and duration of activities and travel. It's also a good idea to keep business cards of contacts you meet and, even better, give a presentation or a report on your trip when you get back to work that includes this information.

👆 TAX FACT

You can claim a deduction for accommodation, food, drink and incidental expenses if you are travelling for work and forced to quarantine due to COVID-19. This concession is not available for returning from personal trips.

There are special substantiation requirements to making a successful travel tax claim.

A travel diary is a separate record of activities undertaken during travel. Its purpose is to show which of the activities were for income-producing purposes so that an appropriate classification can be made between deductible and non-deductible expenses. An activity is recorded by specifying its:

- date and approximate start time
- duration
- location
- nature.

Note that the requirement to keep travel records in the form of a diary is separate from the requirement to obtain written evidence of travel expenses.

👆 TAX FACT

Sometimes taxpayers mix business with pleasure and it is not uncommon to tack on a personal holiday at the end of an overseas conference. However, travel expenses related to attending conferences, seminars and other work-related events are deductible only to the extent that they relate to your income-producing activities.

You will need to apportion your travel expenses where you undertake both work-related and private activities. Travel costs to and from an overseas conference will only be deductible where the main purpose of the travel was to attend the event. Accommodation, food and other incidental costs must be apportioned between work-related and private activities taking into account your activities on the day you incurred the cost.

> **⚠ PITFALL**
>
> Travel expenses for your spouse and family accompanying you while on work-related travel are non-deductible. If any expenses are not separately identifiable, then they will need to be reasonably apportioned between private and deductible.

Some employers pay a travel allowance to cover expenses for accommodation, food, drink or incidentals incurred by an employee while travelling away from home overnight. If your employer does this and the allowance is less than the reasonable travel allowance published by the ATO, you can claim a deduction for the amount of the allowance without further substantiation.

> **⚠ PITFALL**
>
> If you claim an amount greater than the 'reasonable travel allowance amount', the whole claim, not just the excess, must be substantiated.

16 UNIFORM

The cost of certain types of work clothing may be deductible, as may the cost of buying or replacing clothing, uniforms and footwear. But a deduction is only available if the clothing is one of the following:

- protective
- a compulsory uniform to be worn for work
- a non-compulsory uniform that has been entered on the Register of Approved Occupational Clothing.

Tax deductions for the costs of washing, drying or ironing clothes are only available for clothing that falls into one or more of the above categories.

👍 TAX FACT

You can claim the cost of face masks, sanitiser, soap, anti-bacterial sprays and gloves if you purchased these for your protection against COVID in your workplace. However you cannot claim these costs if purchased for your home or other personal purposes such as shopping and entertainment.

👍 TAX FACT

The ATO considers the following to meet the definition of protective clothing:

- fire-resistant and sun-protection clothing
- safety-coloured vests
- non-slip nurse's shoes
- rubber boots for concreters
- steel-capped boots, gloves, overalls, and heavy-duty shirts and trousers
- overalls, smocks and aprons you wear to avoid damage or soiling to your ordinary clothes during your income-earning activities.

If you do your own laundry you can claim $1 per load if the load is made up only of eligible clothes (and includes the washing, drying and ironing of them). This reduces to 50 cents per load if other laundry items are included. If your total laundry costs exceed $150 you must be able to substantiate your claim.

All other expenditure on clothing and its maintenance is considered a private expenditure and is not deductible.

💡 TIP

A deduction for uniformed clothing is only available if it is protective clothing or compulsory, unique and distinctive. Non-compulsory uniforms must be entered on the Register of Approved Occupational Clothing in order to be deductible.

There must be a clear connection between the clothing expenditure and income-earning activities in order to obtain a deduction. In general you cannot claim a deduction for conventional clothing that forms part of a uniform even if your employer requires you to wear it.

✏ EXAMPLE

A businessman wearing a business suit and tie or a sales assistant working for a big fashion label and wearing one of their tops as a condition of employment are not wearing clothes that are deductible.

Clothing purchased by a taxpayer is considered conventional if it is not distinctive or unique, can be worn on any occasion—including private and social occasions—and is easily available to the public.

⚠ PITFALL

Work uniform expenses are a deduction where taxpayers often make mistakes, including:
- not keeping receipts for dry cleaning and uniform purchases to support their claim
- trying to claim for clothing expenses that are conventional and not unique, distinctive or compulsory
- not having a sufficient nexus between their clothing and how it relates to earning income.

17 HOME OFFICE

More and more people these days are doing work at home as an easy remedy to balance the conflicting pressures of work and family. If you perform some of your work from your home office, you may be able to claim a deduction for the costs you incur in running your home office, even if the room is not set aside solely for work-related purposes.

According to the ATO, there are two ways to claim your home office running expenses:

- actual cost method — the work-related portion of your actual expenses
- fixed cost method — a rate of 67 cents per hour (which covers your heating, lighting and cooling, internet, mobile phone, stationery and computer consumables) plus the work-related portion of technology and office furniture such as chairs, desks, computers and bookshelves.

For the actual cost method, you may be able to claim the work-related portion of:

- depreciation of home-office furniture, fittings and equipment such as computers and desks — if your equipment costs less than $300, you can claim a full deduction for the work-related portion
- home telephone calls
- home telephone rental if:
  - you are on call
  - you have to phone your employer, clients or students regularly while you are away from your workplace
- internet access charges
- printer and printer cartridges
- stationery
- the cost of heating, cooling and lighting your home office that is over the amount you would ordinarily have to pay if you did not work from home
- the costs of repairs to your home-office furniture and fittings.

💡 TIP

Although the 67 cents per hour fixed cost method seems like an easy way to work out your home office expenses for your tax return, I estimate that most people will understate their claim by as much as $1500 as they cannot claim internet, mobile phone, home phone and office equipment that they had to incur such as webcams and office furniture nor any stationery or computer consumables. Just like claiming your car expenses, I strongly recommend keeping all of your actual expenses incurred plus your hours worked and choose the best method when you or your tax agent prepares your tax return.

💡 TIP

Sit at your desk at home and scan the room for the various items that you may use, even partially, for work purposes.

✎ EXAMPLE

Shelby uses her computer and personal internet account at home to access her work emails and to grade student assignments in the following percentages:

- 35 per cent for work purposes
- 65 per cent for private purposes.

This means Shelby can claim 35 per cent of both the depreciation of her computer and her internet costs.

⚠ PITFALL

If your income is paid to you as an employee, you are generally not able to claim a deduction for your occupancy expenses including:

- council rates
- home insurance premiums
- mortgage interest
- rent.

You can only claim occupancy expenses where your home office is considered to be a place of business.

Since 1 March 2023, the ATO requires you must keep a diary of the actual number of hours that you work from home in order to claim the fixed rate method for home office expenses.

✏ EXAMPLE

Michelle uses a diary to record the time she uses her home office for work purposes. Based on her diary entries, Michelle works out that she spent 943 hours throughout the year working in her home office.

Under the fixed cost method, Michelle calculates her home-office running expense deduction as follows:

943 hours x 0.67 cents = $632

Michelle could then claim depreciation or repairs and maintenance on any office equipment.

Michelle cannot claim for any additional expenses for home internet, mobile phone, home phone, heating, cooling, lighting, computer consumables nor stationery under the fixed cost method. Alternatively, Michelle could consider calculating the work-related portion of all these costs under the actual costs method.

18 OTHER WORK-RELATED DEDUCTIONS

Other work-related expenses that you incur as an employee that haven't been mentioned previously may include:

- briefcases
- calculators and personal organisers
- diaries and logbooks
- first-aid courses
- income-protection insurances
- interest on money borrowed to finance work-related purchases
- mobile phones

- overtime meal expenses
- postage
- professional seminars, courses, conferences and workshops
- reference books
- stationery
- subscriptions
- sun protection
- technical journals, periodicals and magazines
- tools of trade
- union fees.

⚠ PITFALL

Income protection insurance is great as it can help pay your bills — by paying a percentage of your regular income — if you cannot work due to a sudden illness or injury. It makes sense to insure your income just as you would your house, your car or mobile phone. However there are a few catches to look out for with income protection:

- usually the waiting period is between 14 days and two years, with the lower the waiting period, the higher the premium
- it is generally not available for casual workers, unpaid carers nor part-time employees who work fewer than 20 hours a week
- the benefit period varies from just one year through to age 65, with the longer the period, the more expensive the policy
- whilst the income protection policy is tax deductible, it is only for the portion that directly relates to income protection itself. You cannot claim if it is paid through your superannuation fund nor the portion that relates to a policy that pays a lump sum to compensate for injury (for example, total and permanent disability, life, critical care or trauma)
- if you receive a payment to replace your salary and wages under an income protection policy, you must include it as assessable income in your tax return.

♀ TIP

It is better to get your employer to pay for as many work-related expenses as possible rather than claiming them yourself. Based on the marginal tax rates, you only get back a percentage of any expense incurred, not 100 per cent of the expense. Avoid leaving yourself out of pocket.

If your work-related usage of your telephone is under $50, the ATO will accept your claim based on the following estimates:

- 25 cents per landline call that is work-related
- 75 cents per mobile phone call that is work-related
- 10 cents per text message that is work-related

If your claim for telephone calls exceeds $50 then you must total the overall phone expenditure and apply a work-related percentage based on a representative period of at least four weeks.

✐ EXAMPLE

Lucy uses her mobile phone for work purposes. She is on a mobile phone plan of $49 per month and rarely exceeds the plan cap. She reviews an itemised account for one month from her phone provider, which includes details of the individual calls she has made. She highlights the work-related calls she has made and makes notes on her account about who she is calling for work and personal purposes—her employer, parents, and so on. She works out that 45 per cent of the individual call expenses are for work and applies that to her cap amount of $49 a month. Reviews of other months are consistent with this.

If Lucy only worked for 48 weeks of the year, she would calculate her work-related mobile phone expense deduction as follows:

$$48 \text{ weeks}/52 \text{ weeks} \times 12 \text{ months} \times \$49 \times 0.45 = \$244$$

19 KEEPING THOSE RECEIPTS

It is crucial that you keep your receipts, particularly as the ATO increases its audit activity all the time. With the ATO motto of 'no receipt means no deduction' you could be missing out on legitimate tax deductions by not keeping good records.

Under the Australian tax system of self-assessment you are responsible for working out how much you can claim on your tax return. In order to prepare an accurate tax return and support the claims you make, you need to keep careful records.

Personally I don't care what system you use to keep your receipts ... just have one, although I will say that the ATO have developed an excellent *myDeductions* tool within its ATO app that you could use. The system that works will be organised into various categories to allow you to find a receipt within five minutes if asked.

♀ TIP

If you are struggling to keep a record of your tax deductions during the year, simply download the ATO's *myDeductions* tool within the ATO app to your smart device and make it easier and more convenient at tax time. You can add:

- deductions/expenses
- vehicle trips
- income (if you're a sole trader)
- photos of your invoices and receipts.

Most accountants prefer that you don't give them a shoebox each year, but instead a typed-up summary, perhaps in Excel, of your income and expenses. Their tax agent fees may even fall as a result!

If you're not sure whether or not to keep a record, you should keep it—it is better to have too many than not enough.

♀ TIP

It doesn't matter what system you use to keep your tax receipts, just make sure you use one! An Excel spreadsheet showing your income and expenses works for many people.

If your total claims add up to more than $300, you must keep written evidence, such as receipts, bank statements and credit card statements. You must be able to show evidence you have incurred the full amount of your claim, not just the amount over the first $300.

Written evidence should show:

- amount of the expense
- date you incurred the expense
- nature of the goods or services—if this is not shown, you can write this on the document before you lodge your income tax return
- supplier's name.

If the total amount you are claiming is $300 or less, you do not need to keep receipts.

💡 TIP

In Australia we seem to have an ongoing cycle of natural disasters ranging from floods and drought to catastrophic bushfires and cyclones. Invariably people will only just get enough notice of these devastating weather events to pack only essential items and treasured memories but rarely will they consider to take their tax records. Whilst the ATO will generally provide those affected with extra time to lodge returns and pay outstanding taxes, you will still need to try to reconstruct your tax records as best as possible.

At first instance, contact your bank, your employer, your tax agent and any suppliers of tax-deductible purchases for a copy of information that they would have on file for you. This is where the ATO's *myDeductions* tool within its ATO app becomes invaluable. After exhausting all avenues, if you are still unable to substantiate any claims due to lost or destroyed records, the ATO may still accept your claim/s without substantiation if it's not reasonably possible to obtain the original records.

Generally, you must keep your written evidence for five years from:

- the date the notice of assessment is sent to you
- the date of your last claim for any decline in value for depreciating assets
- disposal of an asset for CGT purposes
- the date a dispute with the ATO is finalised.

🖊 TAX FACT

Taxpayers with 'simple tax affairs' only need to retain their records for two years if:

- their income consists only of salary or wages, interest or dividends within Australia
- deductions are only for managing tax affairs, bank fees or donations.

Documents that you are required to keep can be in written or electronic form. If you make copies they must be a true and clear reproduction of the original.

A PITFALL

> If you keep records electronically, be very careful about not losing that data. A regular back-up is essential to ensure that the evidence is easily accessible if a hard drive is corrupted or a computer stolen.

20 ATO HIT LISTS

Every year, based on an analysis of previous returns, the ATO issues a 'hit list' of occupations that will be targeted for close attention regarding work-related expenses.

TAX FACT

> The ATO's tactic of putting the spotlight on particular groups has proven successful in past years. When the ATO targets particular industries, its tax collection improves by more than 20 per cent.

Generally the ATO looks closely at a range of claims for deductions including expenses for motor vehicles, self-education and travel. It also looks at tax returns from previous years and identifies particular occupations to put under the microscope where:

- average amounts of claims are high
- there is an increase in the number of people making claims
- there are a lot of people making claims for the first time.

In the spirit of 'prevention is much better than cure', the ATO uses that information and writes to people in those occupations. It sends information outlining common mistakes made in claims, and provides help on how people can get their claims right in the subsequent year's tax return.

♀ TIP

While the natural tendency of people in targeted occupations is to reduce the amount of their claims out of fear, if you are genuinely entitled to a legitimate tax deduction then you should claim it. By all means go to the boundary, but not over it. If you are concerned about your claims then you should seek advice from a tax expert.

The first step in a subsequent ATO investigation usually involves a 'please explain' letter requesting further information about your tax return.

Usually a person is given 28 days to respond and the ATO might also ask for copies of receipts and other supporting documents. Only if the matter remains unresolved after this is a face-to-face meeting required.

You will be given lots of opportunity to explain yourself. But the penalties are significant so it's best to have all your affairs in order. Penalties start from a minor adjustment to your return if there was a genuine mistake or misinterpretation of the law, and escalate to severe fines.

⚠ PITFALL

If you make a downright fraudulent claim, say a factory worker claims $20 000 for travel expenses, and there is no substance at all to it, the ATO can charge up to 90 per cent tax in penalties, plus an interest penalty on top of that.

The ATO has outlined some simple rules for getting your work-related expenses claim correct:

- You must have incurred the expense in the year you are claiming for.
- The expense must be work-related and not private.
- Receiving an allowance from your employer does not automatically entitle you to a deduction.
- If your claims total more than $300 you need written evidence.

Penalties that the ATO can charge as a percentage of any tax shortfall are 75 per cent for intentional disregard of a tax law; 50 per cent for recklessness; and 25 per cent when you don't take reasonable care, if your case is not reasonably argued or if you disregard a private ruling by the ATO. If you do not have a tax shortfall, the ATO can charge a fixed dollar amount — $19 800 for intentional disregard; $13 200 for recklessness; or $6600 when you do not take reasonable care.

These penalties are increased by a further 20 per cent of the base amount if you do not cooperate and make it difficult for the ATO when looking at your affairs (for example, the penalty for intentional disregard of a tax law when you don't cooperate becomes 90 per cent, being 120 per cent of the base penalty of 75 per cent). The Commissioner encourages voluntary disclosure so if you confess your sins during an audit investigation they will reduce the base penalty amount by 20 per cent. If you advise of any errors prior to any audit activity, then the base penalty amount is reduced by 80 per cent.

In 2023–24, the ATO spent over $113.95 million on legal costs relating to litigation against taxpayers.

21 REDUNDANCY

Over the past few years there has been plenty of uncertainty in the global economy with many people experiencing job losses from the fallout of COVID-19 coupled with the end of government stimulus measures and the introduction of Donald Trump's 'Liberation Day' tariffs.

If there can be any good news it relates to your favourable tax treatment if you have been dismissed from your employment and received a genuine redundancy payment.

TAX FACT

The ATO has outlined that a genuine redundancy payment is one received by an employee, under age 67, who is dismissed from employment because the employee's position is genuinely redundant and:

- the payment being tested is received because of an employee's termination

- that termination involves the employee being dismissed from employment

- that dismissal is caused by the redundancy of the position

- the redundancy payment is made genuinely because of a redundancy.

Tax-free component of genuine redundancy

Part of a genuine redundancy is tax-free and must be taken in cash. The tax-free limit for the 2025–26 income year is $13100 plus a further $6552 for each completed year of service.

Balance of redundancy

Anything in excess of the tax-free amount is treated as an 'employment termination payment'. The first $260000 in 2025–26 is taxed at 17 per cent if you are 60 and over, or 32 per cent if you are under 60. Any excess payment is taxed at 47 per cent. These tax breaks will only apply to the part of a payment that, when combined with other taxable income, does not exceed $190 000.

Unused leave entitlements

Only 5 per cent of any unused annual or long-service leave that relates to service prior to 16 August 1978 is taxed at your marginal rate. If you leave employment because of a genuine redundancy, invalidity or early retirement scheme, then the balance is taxed at 32 per cent. You cannot roll any unused leave entitlements over into your super fund. Note that the tax calculation on unused leave entitlements is different if you leave employment for any other reason.

✎ EXAMPLE

Natalie, aged 51, is made redundant on 30 June 2026 after working at her company since 15 February 2016. Her company pays her $130 000 as a genuine redundancy plus her unused leave entitlements, which come to another $31 234.

As she has given the company 10 full years of service, the tax-free component of her genuine redundancy is $78 620 ($13 100 + [$6552 × 10]) and the balance of $51 380 is an employment termination payment.

As she is only 51, and doesn't elect to roll over any money into her super fund, the $51 380 is taxed at 32 per cent; that is, $16 442. Her unused leave entitlements are taxed at 32 per cent; that is, $9995.

⚠ PITFALL

While most payroll departments get redundancy and termination calculations correct, occasionally they get them wrong. And when they get them wrong... they can get them horribly wrong. I have seen calculations that have been out by $38 000! It pays to have a tax expert look at the calculations.

22 WORKING A SECOND JOB

Tax problems always seem to occur when you start working a second job. If you are an Australian resident for tax purposes, the first $18 200 of your yearly income is not taxed. This is called the tax-free threshold. You can claim the tax-free threshold from one payer only when you complete your *TFN declaration* (NAT 3092).

You should claim the tax-free threshold with the payer who pays the highest wage. If you earn any additional income from a second job your other payer is required to withhold tax at a higher rate.

If you are currently claiming the tax-free threshold with a payer and you want to claim it from a new payer, you must advise your first payer that you no longer wish to claim the tax-free threshold by completing a withholding declaration (NAT 3093).

⚠ PITFALL

If you claim the tax-free threshold from your second payer it may lead to a tax debt at the end of the financial year. Money can be very hard to find once you have spent it.

Where an insufficient amount of tax is being withheld, you can directly instruct a payer to withhold a higher amount of tax. However, if your payer is withholding tax at the prescribed rates, you are under no obligation to increase the amount of tax being withheld. You suffer no penalty at the end of the financial year, other than having to find a further amount of money to pay your tax.

✏ EXAMPLE

Stuart is employed in two part-time jobs. He receives $30 000 from the first job and $18 000 from the second job and claims the tax-threshold for both jobs. Using the ATO's *Pay-as-you-go (PAYG) withholding—Fortnightly tax table* (NAT 1006), the tax withheld on Stuart's wages is outlined in table 2.1.

▶

TABLE 2.1: example — tax withheld

	Annual income	Fortnightly income	Fortnightly tax
First job	$30000	$1153.85	$84
Second job	$18000	$692.31	$0
Total	$48000	$1846.16	$84

Source: © Australian Taxation Office for the Commonwealth of Australia.

At the end of the financial year Stuart's net tax position is:

Income tax on $48000	$5188
Medicare levy (2%)	$960
Total tax payable	**$6148**
Less: LITO	$280
Less: tax withheld ($84 × 26)	$2184
Net tax shortfall	**$3684**

To avoid this situation, Stuart can either put money aside for when his income tax assessment is issued or choose to ask one or both of his employers to withhold extra tax by not claiming the tax free threshold to cover the shortfall.

If you think you are having too much tax withheld from one of your wages, you can arrange for a PAYG withholding variation form to be completed and reduce the amount withheld from your regular pay. Or wait until the end of the year and get a nice refund.

♀ TIP

When you have a second job you may be able to claim the cost of travelling directly between two separate places of employment. However, you can't claim the cost of travelling from your second job to your home.

23 SALARY SACRIFICE

It is quite common for employees to set up a salary-sacrifice arrangement with their employer and 'package' some of their future salary or wages in return for benefits of a similar value provided by their employer. These benefits may include superannuation and fringe benefits such as company cars, private health insurance and other expense payments.

🖐 TAX FACT

Your income tax liability should be less under a salary-sacrifice arrangement than it would have been without entering into the agreement. It is important to note, though, that there are some associated costs that you need to consider before entering into any arrangement. These costs may include the opportunity cost of the amount being sacrificed plus any surcharges which may arise after having the benefits reported on your payment summary.

Provided that any benefits form part of your remuneration, there is no limit on the amount or the types of benefits that can be sacrificed. They are simply replacing what otherwise could have been paid as salary.

♀ TIP

Superannuation, exempt fringe benefits and some car fringe benefits are generally the best forms of salary sacrifice for tax purposes.

Salary-sacrificed superannuation contributions under an effective salary-sacrifice arrangement are considered to be employer contributions and are taxed at 15 per cent (increasing to 30 per cent for individuals with income greater than $250 000), subject to contribution limits, within the fund. This is a lot more tax-effective than paying 47 per cent tax on your cash salary, if you are on the highest marginal tax rate.

Make sure that you agree to all the terms of any salary-sacrifice arrangement with your employer, preferably in writing and before starting any work. A contract of employment is a good place to detail the arrangement. You can renegotiate a salary-sacrifice arrangement at any time, such as in renewable contracts.

The ATO is known to frown upon any arrangements put into place after the work has been performed, and arrangements that are not in writing. You are allowed to have a verbal agreement but you may have difficulty establishing the facts of your arrangement should the tax man conduct an audit of your affairs.

Salary sacrifice implications for employees include:

- Income tax is paid on the reduced salary or wages.
- Your employer may be liable to pay fringe benefits tax (FBT) on the non-cash benefits they provide and is likely to adjust your remuneration accordingly.
- Salary-sacrificed superannuation contributions are classified as employer superannuation contributions (rather than employee contributions) and are taxed at 15 per cent in the superannuation fund (increasing to 30 per cent for individuals with income greater than $250 000).
- There should be no access to the sacrificed salary; it must be permanently forgone for the period of the arrangement.
- Your employer may be required to report certain benefits on your payment summary that also need to be disclosed in your annual income tax return.

24 FRINGE BENEFITS

A fringe benefit is a benefit either you or an associate, such as your spouse or children, receive because of your employment. If there is any fringe benefit tax (FBT) payable on the benefits received, your employer is liable to pay that tax. You only pay income tax on your reduced salary. But as part of your salary–sacrifice agreement your salary may be reduced by the amount of FBT paid by your employer.

Common fringe benefits include:

- car parking
- cars
- expense payments
- housing
- loans
- meals and entertainment
- property.

👍 **TAX FACT**

Employees of certain not-for-profit organisations receive generous FBT concessions. The FBT cap on exempt benefits provided by public and not-for-profit hospitals and public ambulances is $17 000. This cap increases to $30 000 for public benevolent institutions (except hospitals) and health promotion charities.

The following — limited to one per year — are exempt benefits:

- briefcase
- computer software
- portable electronic device (unlimited for small businesses)
- protective clothing
- tools of the trade.

There are two alternative methods to calculate the FBT for cars:

- Logbook — based on actual usage over a 12-week period completed in the past five years.
- Statutory method — a flat rate of 20 per cent for all cars acquired after 1 April 2014.

Due to the high cost of FBT, most employers elect to pay employees a car allowance in the vicinity of $15 000 to $20 000. While this allowance is taxable, you can claim the work-related portion of the various running costs as a deduction (see p. 33). Rather than waiting until year end for a big refund once your return has been lodged, to reduce the amount of tax in your periodic pay, submit a PAYG Withholding Variation and get the tax benefit upfront (see p. 111).

Ways to reduce FBT may include the following:

- Make an employee contribution towards the cost of the benefit.
- Keep a logbook.
- For cars acquired before 10 May 2011, travel more and get into a lower statutory fraction bracket.
- Consider getting a commercial vehicle (exempt).
- Return the car and keys to your employer when you are not using the car for extended periods, such as holidays.

♀ TIP

Consider salary packaging an electric car and avoid paying fringe benefits tax. You do not pay FBT if the car is a zero or low emissions vehicle which was first purchased after 30 June 2022 and luxury car tax has never been payable on the car. The luxury car threshold for fuel efficient vehicles is $91387 compared to $80567 for other vehicles. From 1 July 2025 plug-in hybrid electric vehicles will not be eligible for this exemption.

Reportable fringe benefits amounts are certain fringe benefits greater than $2000 which are included in your payment summary and shown in your tax return, but not included in your assessable income. They are included in a number of income tests for certain government benefits including:

- Medicare levy surcharge
- deductions for personal super contributions
- super co-contributions
- spouse super contributions
- HELP and Financial Supplement repayments
- child-support obligations.

✋ TAX FACT

The FBT record keeping exemption threshold is $10664 for the FBT year ending 31 March 2026.

✏ EXAMPLE

Table 2.2 illustrates the way salary sacrificing and employee contributions work. Aaron earns $74000 a year. He has a car purchased for $40000 which has annual running expenses of $15000. If he travels 22000 kilometres during the FBT year, the taxable value of the car fringe benefit will be $8000 (20 per cent × $40000) and he will need to sacrifice one of the following:

- $22094 without any employee contributions
- $7000 if employee contributions of $8000 are made.

▶

TABLE 2.2: example — salary sacrifice

	1 Salary only (no packaging)	2 Salary + car (without employee contributions)	3 Salary + car (with employee contributions)
Annual remuneration	$74 000	$74 000	$74 000
Less salary sacrifice	Nil	$22 094	$7000
Taxable income	**$74 000**	**$51 906**	**$67 000**
Less income tax	$12 988	$6360	$10 888
Less Medicare levy	$1480	$1038	$1340
Add LITO	Nil	$221	Nil
Income after tax/ salary sacrifice	**$59 532**	**$44 729**	**$54 772**
Less employee contribution	Nil	Nil	$8000
Less car expenses	$15 000	Nil	Nil
Net disposable income	**$44 532**	**$44 729**	**$46 772**
Reportable fringe benefits amount (taxable value × 1.8868)	Nil	$15 094	Nil

Source: © Australian Taxation Office for the Commonwealth of Australia.

⚠ PITFALL

There is a grossed-up $5000 cap on the amount of salary-sacrificed 'meal entertainment' and 'entertainment facility leasing expenses' which qualify for an FBT exemption or rebate.

25 LIVING-AWAY-FROM-HOME ALLOWANCE

The ATO defines a living-away-from-home allowance (LAFHA) as a taxable allowance that an employer pays to an employee to compensate for additional expenses incurred and any disadvantages suffered because the employee is required to live away from their usual place of residence in order to perform their employment-related duties.

You are considered to be living away from your usual place of residence when:

- you change your job location (but not your employer)
- you intend to return to your original location after time away
- the period away exceeds 21 days.

As a practical general rule, where the period away does not exceed 21 days, the allowance will be treated as a travelling allowance rather than as a LAFHA.

FBT is only payable on the amount that the LAFHA exceeds the exempt accommodation and food components.

👍 TAX FACT

Working holiday makers (that is, backpackers with either 417 or 462 visa subclass) are taxed at 15 per cent for the first $45000 of their income. As table 2.3 shows, the subsequent 'backpacker tax' is at the same rates as residents on incomes above $45000.

TABLE 2.3: tax rates for working holiday makers excluding levies (2025–26)

Taxable income	Tax on this income
$0–$45000	15c for each $1
$45001–$135000	$6750 plus 30c for each $1 over $45000
$135001–$190000	$33750 plus 37c for each $1 over $135000
$190001 and over	$54100 plus 45c for each $1 over $190000

Source: © Australian Taxation Office for the Commonwealth of Australia.

LAFHA can only be claimed by people who maintain a home for their own use in Australia that they are living away from for work. In addition, the LAFHA concession can only be used for the expenses of people who are legitimately maintaining a second home in addition to their actual home for a maximum period of 12 months. For those Australian residents who had an employment arrangement in place before 8 May 2012 (that has not been materially varied), then the LAFHA rules that have been applicable since 1 July 2014.

You have not made a material change to your employment arrangement if:

• your salary is adjusted as a result of an annual salary review (or other annual adjustments are made)
• you are promoted and the underlying terms of your employment arrangement do not change.

Accommodation

The exempt accommodation component of the LAFHA is the amount you pay for additional accommodation expenses you could reasonably be expected to incur at the alternative location. The ATO doesn't have any strict guidelines concerning what is considered 'reasonable accommodation', but it mainly boils down to common sense. Factors you could take into account when determining the accommodation cost include:

• whether you will be accompanied by family members
• the position you hold
• the location where you will be living
• whether the accommodation will be furnished
• your current living standards.

⚠ PITFALL

If an employee does not spend all of the LAFHA provided for accommodation, the excess is not an exempt accommodation component and is taxable for FBT purposes.

Food

The exempt food component is the amount of the LAFHA that is compensation for expenses you could reasonably be expected to incur on food and drink because you must live away from your usual place of residence, less the statutory food amount of $42 a week for each adult (12 years old and above) and $21 a week for each child (under 12 at the beginning of the year).

♦ TAX FACT

There are no strict guidelines as to how the food component is calculated, provided the amount is reasonable. You could determine reasonable food costs using the rates the ATO publishes each year for expatriates, providing they are reasonable in your circumstances. The acceptable amounts for the reasonable food component in the 2025–26 financial year of LAFHAs within Australia for employees, per ATO Tax Determination 2025/2, are as follows:

- one adult $341
- two adults $512
- three adults $683
- one adult + one child $427
- two adults + one child $598
- two adults + two children $684
- two adults + three children $770
- three adults + one child $769
- three adults + two children $855
- four adults $854
- additional adult $171
- additional child $86.

The reasonable food and drinks amounts for a LAFHA paid to employees living outside of Australia per ATO Tax Determination 2025/2 vary by six broad categories of countries, as outlined in table 2.4 (overleaf).

TABLE 2.4: reasonable food and drinks amounts for a LAFHA paid per week to one adult employee living outside of Australia (2025–26)

Country cost group	Reasonable weekly amount	Example of countries include
1	$173	Cambodia, Iran
2	$237	Argentina, Sudan, Tunisia
3	$319	India, Philippines, Sri Lanka
4	$392	Bangladesh, Canada, NZ, Portugal
5	$528	Japan, USA, UK
6	$656	Singapore, Switzerland, UAE

Source: © Australian Taxation Office for the Commonwealth of Australia.

Where the employee is accompanied by other family members whilst working overseas, the above reasonable food and drink amounts is increased by 50 per cent for each additional adult and 25 per cent for each additional child.

⚠ PITFALL

457 visa holders do not satisfy the requirement of maintaining a home for their own use in Australia while they are living away from it. As a result, they are not able to claim deductions for accommodation and food, but will still need to include any allowance received as assessable income.

✦ TAX FACT

If you are an employee who works on a 'fly-in fly-out' or a 'drive-in drive-out' basis (such as a miner), then you are not subject to the same 'maximum 12 months' LAFHA rule. You will still need to substantiate your accommodation and food expenses if they are more than the ATO's reasonable amounts.

PART III
YOUR EDUCATION

Contrary to what many property experts and stockbrokers may tell you, the best investment that you could make is in yourself. With the economy recovering there are going to be some great opportunities in the job market for those who have acquired more skills. You are never too old to learn new tricks and, as my old man would say, nobody can take your education away from you.

👆 TAX FACT

Of the 599 000 taxpayers that claimed for self-education expenses in 2021–22, 69 per cent earned less than $100 000 for the year.

Australia is in the midst of an education revolution and pushing for more highly skilled workers. Tax and government incentives are helping fill the classrooms of universities and technical and further education (TAFE) colleges around the country with part-time students every evening. Employers are also expecting more from their employees and encouraging them to study in conjunction with their work.

💡 TIP

If you are planning to claim self-education expenses, be sure that the course you are claiming specifically relates to a current income-producing role, not one you hope to have in the future.

This part focuses on the financial implications and government incentives around studying.

26 CLAIMING SELF-EDUCATION EXPENSES

Work-related self-education expenses are the costs you incur to undertake a work-related course of study at a school, college, university or other recognised place of education.

👆 TAX FACT

The ATO says a tax deduction for your self-education expenses is available if you work and study at the same time, the course has sufficient connection to your current employment, and it *either*:

- maintains or improves the specific skills or knowledge you require in your current employment

  or
- results in, or is likely to result in, an increase in your income from your current employment.

According to the ATO, if a course of study is too general in terms of your current income-earning activities, the necessary connection between the self-education expense and your income-earning activity does not exist.

⚠ PITFALL

The ATO is quite strict in its view on self-education expense deductions. A deduction for self-education expenses cannot be claimed for a course that does not have a sufficient connection to your current employment even if the course:

- is generally related to your current employment
- enables you to get new employment.

Provided there is sufficient connection between your course and employment at the time you incurred the expense, the following self-education expenses are allowable tax deductions:

- accommodation and meals, only when participating in your course requires you to be away from home for one or more nights
- computer expenses, including interest to finance them
- depreciation of the cost of your computer, professional libraries, desks, chairs, filing cabinets, bookshelves, calculators, technical instruments, tools and other equipment (such as desk lamps)
- photocopying
- running expenses if you have a room set aside for work-related study purposes—such as the cost of heating, cooling and lighting that room while you are studying in it
- self-education expenses paid with your Overseas Study— Higher Education Loan Program (OS-HELP) loan
- stationery
- student union fees
- textbooks, professional and trade journals
- travel expenses between your home (or work) to your place of education and back
- tuition fees, including fees payable under FEE-HELP.

♀ TIP

If you have a room set aside for work-related study purposes, you can claim a fixed rate of 67 cents per hour of usage plus the decline in value of office furniture and equipment rather than keep individual costs of heating, cooling, lighting, internet, consumables and phone usage.

You cannot claim a tax deduction for:

- accommodation and meals associated with day-to-day living expenses
- repayments you make (whether compulsory or voluntary) on debts you may have under the following loan schemes:
  - HECS-HELP
  - FEE-HELP

- OS-HELP
- Student Financial Supplement Scheme (SFSS)
- self-education expenses such as tuition fees paid under HECS-HELP
- last stage of your travel between home, work and place of education.

Self-development courses

Over the past few decades we have seen a rise in the number of self-development courses that cover a range of different topics, most of which are not tax-deductible. Just like with university and TAFE courses, the ATO will only allow you to claim a deduction for expenses relating to courses that have a sufficient nexus with your income-producing activities.

There has also been a dramatic increase in the number of 'success seminars' where thousands sit in an audience for one or two days and listen to a presenter on the big stage. They are short, intense programs without the active involvement that would be expected from a TAFE or uni student. As a result, the ATO considers the material covered by these seminars as being too generic and not specific enough to a taxpayer's income-earning activities.

Some topics are clearly private in nature, such as diet and nutrition, intimate relations and meditation.

Likewise, self-development courses can have a strong philosophical or spiritual component, can be undertaken over months or years and can often be offered by correspondence.

⚠ PITFALL

Fees for courses on personal development or life-coaching programs are not generally deductible as the link between your current employment and the program is not clear enough—the course is considered to be essentially personal in nature.

Other topics are too general in scope to be classed as income-related, such as communication skills, decision making and getting along with others.

The ATO outlines that to be eligible for a deduction for expenses you incur for a self-improvement or personal development course, the course must have a sufficient connection to your current employment and *either:*

- maintain or improve the specific skills/knowledge you require in your current employment

  or

- result in, or be likely to result in, an increase in your income from your current employment.

Personal or executive coaching may be considered income-related if the series of regular discussions between the participant and a coach have a strong income-related focus. If the program has a strong focus on finding the participants' goals and directions, and on their work–life balance, then income-related material is barely covered.

The amount of the deduction you can claim will be determined by the extent to which the course is directly related to your current income-earning activities.

✎ EXAMPLE

Suzie is a manager who undertakes a self-development course consisting of the following five modules, all of equal value and cost:

- communication
- getting on with others
- handling change
- leadership
- mediation.

The module on leadership would be classed as income-related, but the remainder of the modules are private or too general in nature to be tax-deductible. As the income-related content makes up 20 per cent of the course, Suzie can only claim a deduction for 20 per cent of the costs that she incurs in undertaking the course.

---

27 STUDENT LOANS

There are a number of government benefits that provide financial assistance while you are studying either at university or doing a trade.

Higher Education Loan Program

University students are generally a pretty poor bunch who struggle to pay for next week's rent, let alone their course fees. So the Higher Education Loan Program (HELP) was introduced to provide a loan to assist students to pay for their university tuition.

While there is no interest rate as such, an adjustment is effectively charged on HELP debts at the lower of the Consumer Price Index (CPI) or the Wage Price Index (WPI) on 1 June each year. According to the ATO, the average HELP debt among 2.932 million taxpayers is $27 641.

Once you start working and your income is above a minimum repayment threshold, you must make compulsory repayments, which the ATO works out via your income tax assessment, as outlined in table 3.1. On 1 July each year, these HELP repayment thresholds are indexed by the lower of the CPI or WPI.

> **👆 TAX FACT**
>
> For debts incurred after 1 January 2020, a combined lifetime HELP limit of $182172 applies to students studying medicine, dentistry, veterinary science and selected aviation courses, reducing to $126839 for other students. Any FEE-HELP, VET FEE-HELP and VET Student Loan debts prior to 2020 are carried forward and count towards your HELP loan limit.

TABLE 3.1: HELP repayment thresholds and rates (2024–25)

HELP repayment income (HRI*)	Repayment rate
Below $54 435	Nil
$54 435–$62 850	1.00%
$62 851–$66 620	2.00%
$66 621–$70 618	2.50%
$70 619–$74 855	3.00%
$74 856–$79 346	3.50%
$79 347–$84 107	4.00%
$84 108–$89 154	4.50%
$89 155–$94 503	5.00%
$94 504–$100 174	5.50%
$100 175–$106 185	6.00%
$106 186–$112 556	6.50%
$112 557–$119 309	7.00%
$119 310–$126 467	7.50%
$126 468–$134 056	8.00%
$134 057–$142 100	8.50%
$142 101–$150 626	9.00%
$150 627–$159 663	9.50%
$159 664 and above	10.00%

*HRI = taxable income plus any total net investment loss (which includes net rental losses), total reportable fringe benefits amounts, reportable super contributions and exempt foreign employment income.

Source: © Australian Taxation Office for the Commonwealth of Australia.

📢 PROPOSED CHANGE

The 2025–26 federal budget proposed the raising of the minimum repayment threshold from $54 435 to $67 000 and reducing repayment rates by calculating repayments only on the income above the new $67 000 threshold. It was also proposed that all study and training support loans to be reduced on 1 June 2025 by 20 per cent.

💡 TIP

If you only work full time during university holidays or part time while studying, then ask your employer not to withhold additional amounts for HELP or SFSS debts (see p. 74), provided that you do not expect to earn above the annual repayment thresholds. If your employer continues to deduct these amounts, then you should lodge your income tax return as soon as possible in order to get your tax refund quickly.

👆 TAX FACT

HELP debts are not extinguished if you go overseas or become bankrupt. Even on death, the executor of your estate must lodge all outstanding tax returns and the estate is liable for any compulsory repayments that relate to the period before your death. Only then is the remainder of the accumulated debt cancelled by the ATO.

⚠ PITFALL

If you're thinking of heading overseas to avoid having to repay your HELP debt then think again. The ATO will request compulsory repayments based on worldwide income derived in an Australian income tax year. Non-residents will need to notify the ATO of their contact details and lodge a worldwide income report upon which compulsory HELP repayment calculations will be based.

? FAQ

I have a HELP debt and am working two jobs while I study but I expect to earn only $25 000 from those jobs (well under the threshold for needing to make a HELP repayment) although for my second job, they are withholding approximately $150 each fortnight from my pay. Will I get all this back when I lodge my tax return and will the ATO see that I have earned under the threshold?

As your income will be under the repayment threshold, the ATO will not calculate any HELP debt repayments when they assess you at the end of the year. That may not necessarily mean that you will get a nice refund at the end of the year because the $150 tax being deducted each fortnight is going into a general pool of tax deducted. If enough tax is not being taken out of the second job (due to double claiming the tax-free threshold, as an example) then the ATO will use the excess HELP deductions to cover this shortfall.

Student Financial Supplement Scheme

The Student Financial Supplement Scheme (SFSS) was a voluntary loan scheme to help tertiary students cover their expenses while studying. While the scheme was closed in 2003, the ATO continues to collect existing financial supplement debts through the tax system.

As with HELP debts, an adjustment is effectively charged on SFSS debts based on the lower of CPI or WPI on 1 June each year. Once you no longer have a HELP debt, the repayment rates and thresholds for your SFSS debt are the same as those shown for HELP in table 3.2. There will be no repayment required for the SFSS debt whilst you have a HELP debt.

👆 TAX FACT

SFSS loans are repaid after the repayment of HELP loans based on the HELP repayment thresholds.

Like it is for HELP debts, there is no bonus if you make a voluntary repayment against your SFSS debt.

? FAQ

I have an SFSS debt. If I die, does my debt get passed to my next of kin or is it voided completely?

Your estate will need to lodge a final 'date of death' tax return and repayments for SFSS will be calculated normally as in any other tax year. However, you can die peacefully knowing that any remaining SFSS (or HELP) debt will be written off by the government and you will not be leaving any huge debts to your family.

Australian Apprenticeship Support Loans

Previously called Trade Support Loans this program was introduced in 2014 to encourage more young people to commence a trade and complete their qualification.

Eligible Australian apprentices can receive a lifetime loan limit of $25 374 (indexed with inflation on 1 July each year) over four years to assist with everyday costs while they complete their apprenticeship over a four-year period.

To be eligible for Australian Apprenticeship Support Loans payments, apprentices must:

- reside in Australia and be an Australian citizen, or the holder of a permanent visa;
- be undertaking a:
  - Certificate III or IV level qualification that leads to an occupation on the National Skills Needs List; or
  - Certificate II, III or IV agricultural qualification; or
  - Certificate II, III or IV horticulture qualification while working in rural or regional Australia; and

- meet the eligibility criteria that is assessed by the Australian Apprenticeships Centre on receipt of an Australian Apprenticeship Support Loan Application Form.

There are no age restrictions for applying for an Australian Apprenticeship Support Loan.

TAX FACT

Under the Australian Apprenticeship Support Loan program, eligible Australian apprentices can access up to $10150 in their first year, $7612 in the second, $5075 in the third and $2537 in the fourth year. If apprentices have not reached their $25374 lifetime limit after four years, they may also receive up to $2537 per annum in subsequent years.

♀ TIP

Upon successful completion of an apprenticeship, Australian apprentices will be entitled to a 20 per cent discount on the loan. Now that is an incentive to knuckle down and get your trade.

Similar to HELP loans for tertiary students, the loans become repayable once apprentices start earning a particular amount of worldwide income.

The Australian Apprenticeship Support Loan debt is repaid through the tax system once your repayment income is above the minimum repayment threshold for compulsory repayment.

The repayment rates and thresholds are the same as those for the Higher Education Loan Program (HELP). For the 2024–25 income year, the minimum repayment threshold is $54434 (proposed to increase to $67000 from 1 July 2025).

TAX FACT

The Australian Apprenticeship Support Loans program is administered by the Australian Apprenticeships Centre and the Department of Employment and Workplace Relations. For more information go to www.apprenticeships.gov.au

FEE-HELP

FEE-HELP is a loan for eligible fee-paying students enrolled at an eligible higher education provider or Open Universities of Australia.

☛ TAX FACT

For 2025, the combined lifetime limit for all tuition fee assistance under HECS-HELP, FEE-HELP, VET FEE-HELP and VET Student Loans is $126 839 for most students increasing to $182 172 for students undertaking medicine, dentistry, veterinary science and selected aviation courses. You can check your available borrowing and HELP balance via the myHELPbalance portal www.myhelpbalance.gov.au.

VET Student Loans

The Vocational Education and Training (VET) student loans program is an income contingent loan offered by the Government to assist eligible students undertaking certain VET diploma, advanced diploma, graduate diploma and graduate certificate courses of study at an approved VET provider.

♀ TIP

If you take out a FEE-HELP or VET student loan to pay your tuition fees, you may be entitled to a tax deduction for the cost of your tuition fees.

OS-HELP

Overseas Study HELP (OS-HELP) is a loan that helps students meet airfares, accommodation costs and other travel expenses while undertaking some of their study overseas.

♀ TIP

If you take out an OS-HELP loan to pay costs associated with overseas study, you may be entitled to claim a tax deduction for some of the costs.

🎁 BONUS RESOURCES

If you want to check your HELP limit and available HELP balance you can visit the *myHELP* portal at www.myHELPbalance.gov.au

28 AUSTUDY AND ABSTUDY

Austudy

Austudy is a government benefit paid by Centrelink that provides financial help for students and apprentices. If you are either studying an approved full-time course at an approved institution or undertaking a full-time Australian apprenticeship and are aged 25 or over, then you may be eligible for Austudy. Approved courses for Austudy purposes include full-time secondary education courses, graduate courses, undergraduate courses and some masters, diplomas and TAFE courses. If you have already completed a masters degree or a doctorate, then this is likely to disqualify you from any payment, regardless of satisfying the above criteria. Both income and assets tests need to be satisfied in order to receive Austudy. Unlike the Youth Allowance, there is no parental means test requirement.

Income test

You can earn up to $528 per fortnight (before tax) and receive the full Austudy entitlement. The payment is reduced by 50 cents in the dollar if your income is between $529 and $633 and by 60 cents in the dollar when you earn above $633 per fortnight. If you are receiving Austudy, you must report your employment income to Centrelink every fortnight, even if you are not paid in some fortnights.

Assets test

As an applicant for Austudy you will be assessed against an assets test, depending on age and home-ownership.

Single homeowners must have assets other than their home worth less than $314 000 in order to satisfy the assets test for Austudy entitlements (and most other government allowances and pensions), rising to $566 000 for single non-homeowners. For couples, the combined assets limit is $470 000 for those who own a home, rising to $722 000 for those who do not. These couples limits also apply where illness may separate spouses.

♀ TIP

Visit the Services Australia website www.servicesaustralia.gov.au for the most up-to-date information on the asset test limits for allowances and full pension entitlements. Figures are updated four times each year, in January, March, July and September.

Austudy is not payable if your assets exceed these amounts. Even if you satisfy the assets test, payments may still be deferred if your liquid assets (such as cash, shares and term deposits) exceed $5500 if you are single, or $11 000 if you are a couple or single with dependants.

♦ TAX FACT

There are other government payments and benefits that you may be entitled to if you receive Austudy, including:

- advance payment
- fares allowance
- low-income health care card

- pharmaceutical allowance
- remote area allowance
- rent assistance
- student start-up scholarship.

ABSTUDY

ABSTUDY is a government allowance that is similar to Austudy and is available to Indigenous secondary or tertiary students or full-time Australian apprentices, as an incentive to stay at school or in further study. Those students and apprentices of Australian Aboriginal or Torres Strait Islander descent or who identify as an Aboriginal or Torres Strait Islander person (and are accepted as such by their community) may be eligible for ABSTUDY.

⚠ PITFALL

A tax deduction for self-education expenses is not available if the only income you received was from one of the following:

- Austudy
- ABSTUDY
- similar payments providing financial assistance.

✋ TAX FACT

The ATO will not allow any deduction for self-education expenses against any government assistance payments, including Austudy and ABSTUDY.

🎁 BONUS RESOURCES

If you wish to check your eligibility for Austudy or ABSTUDY, go to your Centrelink online account which you can link via your myGov account. Visit my.gov.au for more information.

29 SCHOLARSHIPS

How scholarships are structured will determine if they are taxable or tax-free.

Scholarships are exempt from income tax when a full-time student at a school, college or university receives a stipend for a scholarship, bursary, educational allowance or other educational assistance.

However, the principal purpose of the scholarship must be the education of the student.

🖕 TAX FACT

Scholarship payments are exempt from income tax if:

- they are made to a full-time student at a school, college, TAFE or university
- they are made by way of scholarship, bursary, educational allowance or educational assistance
- it is accepted that selection to receive a scholarship is merit-based and that the scholarship has the requisite educational purpose.

⚠ PITFALL

Beware of promoters who offer to help you set up a scholarship fund to pay for your children's education with the promise that the arrangement will minimise your tax. The ATO has announced that these arrangements are not genuine scholarships as students are not independently selected on a wide range of criteria and that any scholarship payments under these arrangements are taxable in the hands of the student.

Some scholarships, bursaries, grants and awards are taxable, including education benefits provided under a friendly society scholarship plan.

🖕 TAX FACT

Scholarship payments are subject to income tax if they are payments made:

- by the Commonwealth for education or training
- to part-time students

- under a scholarship that does not have merit-based selection
- on condition that the student will (or will if required) become an employee of the payer
- on condition that the student will (or will if required) enter into a contract with the payer that is wholly or principally for the labour of the student
- under a scholarship that is not provided principally for educational purposes.

If you are not sure about the tax consequences of a scholarship payment, contact the organisation that paid you.

🍐 TAX FACT

If your scholarship is taxable you should advise your payer that your scholarship is assessable income — they will need to withhold tax (PAYG) from your periodic payments. You will need to show your scholarship amount as assessable income in your tax return.

⚠ PITFALL

If you have a family trust and distribute some of the net income to your child's school to cover their school fees then do so at your peril. The ATO views these transactions as a way to try and avoid tax and will generally assess tax on the trustees of the family trust at 47 per cent of the amount paid to the school.

30 SCHOOL BUILDING FUNDS

Many parents make payments to school building funds but they are not necessarily tax-deductible.

For a gift to a school building fund to qualify for a tax deduction, it must have the following characteristics:

- made voluntarily
- amounts to $2 or more

- made to a school building fund that is endorsed as a deductible gift recipient (DGR)
- made to a school building fund that is maintained solely for providing money for acquiring, constructing or maintaining the school or college buildings
- put towards a building, or group of buildings, used for a purpose that is connected with the curriculum of a school or college by a non-profit organisation
- does not provide a material benefit to the donor (such as a reduction in school fees, tickets to functions or the grant of scholarships to nominated students)
- essentially arises from benefaction.

⚠ PITFALL

Compulsory payments to a school building fund are not deductible. They are essentially a levy and part of the total school fees.

The ATO will not allow deductions for building funds that are for sports grounds, tennis courts, covered play areas, car parks, landscaping, furniture or equipment. However, the ATO would allow deductions relating to the building of an indoor sports complex on school grounds (where it includes a gym, basketball court and an in-ground swimming pool) as it is a permanent structure forming an enclosure providing protection from the elements.

A multipurpose building is taken to be used as a school or college if the primary and principal use of the building (more than 50 per cent of the time) is as a school or college.

✎ EXAMPLE

A hall used by a school every weekday by students and teachers and for community meetings at weekends would qualify as a school or college building. If the hall was used as a basketball court for external groups only it would not be considered a school or college building.

Donors need to keep records of their deductible gifts for tax record-keeping purposes. Receipts for gifts must state the name of the fund, authority or institution to which the gift has been made, the DGR's Australian business number (if any) and the fact that the receipt is for a gift.

✏ EXAMPLE

Alain voluntarily gives $700 cash to a school building fund that is a DGR. He can claim an income tax deduction for $700 because:

- it is made to a DGR
- the payment is a gift
- a payment of money falls within one of the gift types
- there are no gift conditions for school building funds.

⚠ PITFALL

A deduction for a gift to a school building fund cannot add to or create a tax loss for a taxpayer.

☝ TAX FACT

Over 4.26 million individuals claimed over $4.55 billion in donations in the 2021–22 financial year. As at March 2025, there were 63 070 registered charities in Australia of which 39 per cent were deductible gift recipients.

🎁 BONUS RESOURCES

For more information for people wanting to claim a tax deduction for gifts to school building funds (or for organisations wanting to establish them), look up the ATO's Taxation Ruling *TR 2013/2 Income tax: school or college building funds.*

31 EDUCATION SAVINGS PLANS

Having a savings plan for your kids' education is a brilliant idea and something that every responsible parent should start as early as possible. As you probably already know, the cost of raising and educating a family isn't cheap.

💡 TIP

Friendly societies usually issue education savings plans. They are great in terms of creating discipline (by encouraging regular deposits and restricting withdrawals) and they can be tax-effective. However, check their investment returns prior to investing because sometimes they can be poor.

In order to be tax-free, education savings plans need to be issued for the sole purpose of providing 'education benefits' for nominated students and not used as security for borrowing or raising money.

Any withdrawals of funds that relate to contributions made are considered capital in nature and therefore tax-free. However, the student must include in their assessable income any withdrawals of funds that relate to investment income on those contributions. With the higher tax-free threshold and the low-income tax offset, it would be expected that there would be no tax to pay on any payments made to students in the year that they turn 18 (and subsequent years) as they are assessed under adult tax rates.

Benefits that are withdrawn and used for an expense that is not directly related to the nominated student's education will be treated as 'non-education benefits'. In that event, the ATO deems the recipient to be the member and not the nominated student. This benefit will be treated similarly to the proceeds of a 10-year bond, for which the following rules apply:

- No personal tax is payable on withdrawals after 10 years subject to a 125 per cent further contributions tax rule (where the total amount of contributions paid during a year increases by no more than 125 per cent of the total contributions in the previous year).
- If a withdrawal is in the first eight years, the growth component is assessable but a 30 per cent tax offset applies to offset the personal tax impact.
- If the withdrawal is within the ninth year, only two-thirds of the growth is assessable, with only one-third assessable if withdrawn in the tenth year. The 30 per cent tax rebate is also available on withdrawals in those years, and is calculated on the assessable portion.

PART IV

YOUR INVESTMENT PROPERTY

Almost one in every four taxpayers in Australia owns a rental property. Aside from increasing their financial wealth, many people invest in property to enjoy the tax benefits.

☝ TAX FACT

Over 2.27 million people claimed more than $44.41 billion in rental deductions in their tax returns in the 2021–22 tax year.

While rental income is assessable, outgoings relating to your investment property are allowable deductions and can be offset against other income. This will generally result in a tax refund for the taxpayer. So the more that you can claim as allowable deductions, the lower your taxable income becomes and the higher your refund.

♀ TIP

If you own a rental property with someone else, you need to show your share of the rental income and expenses in your income tax return in the same proportion as shown on the legal title of the property.

For those who proceed down the investment property track, a big part of the available tax deduction is the interest portion of the mortgage.

Other costs that can be claimed include property management fees, rates, loan costs and maintenance and repairs.

In part IV we will focus on how to maximise the tax benefits of owning a rental property as well as looking at ways to minimise any CGT liability in the future.

As you will see, deductions for investment properties can be quite substantial and generate large tax refunds, particularly if a property doesn't generate much rent by comparison. However, the property must be rented, or 'genuinely available' for rental, in the income year for which you claim a deduction. If you start to use the property for private purposes, you cannot claim any interest expenses you incur after you start using the property for private purposes.

♀ TIP

It is very important that you have a clear intention of renting your property. If you make no attempt to advertise your property or set the rent unrealistically high, the ATO will find that you have no intention of renting your property and your rental claims may not be allowed.

In some situations, rental expenses may need to be apportioned. For example, if your holiday home is used by you, your friends or your relatives free of charge for part of the year, you are not entitled to a deduction for costs incurred during those periods.

♦ TAX FACT

If you rent your property to family or friends at below market rent, the ATO may treat this as a 'private' arrangement and only allow you to claim sufficient deductions to offset the rent, but not enough to make a tax loss.

Be careful not to overstate interest deductions where the loan is partly for private purposes, such as claiming interest on a holiday house property where it is used, say for one month (one-twelfth), by your family for holidays.

Rental properties have been on the ATO's watch list for a few years now because the sizes of the tax deductions are significant and they are a haven for errors. Each year, the ATO makes contact with many thousands of taxpayers with rental properties and asks them to explain and justify what they put in their tax return. Make sure that you can justify your claim.

Common mistakes include not having a depreciation schedule from a quantity surveyor, adding back personal usage of property, making a deduction for travel expenses and claiming capital items as repairs.

For more information on how rental income and expenses are treated for tax purposes, the ATO has an excellent publication titled Rental properties (NAT 1729).

32 NEGATIVE GEARING

When expenses relating to an investment property (such as rates, insurance, repairs and interest) are greater than the rent you receive then you are negatively gearing it. The net loss is a deduction in your tax return—against other income such as salary, interest and business income—and will generally result in a refund.

Table 4.1 is an example of how to calculate your net rental income or loss.

TABLE 4.1: net rental income or loss

	Scenario 1	Scenario 2	Scenario 3	Scenario 4
(a) Assessable income before rent	$220000	$150000	$70000	$35000
Rental income	$9300	$9300	$9300	$9300
Rental expense	$20600	$20600	$20600	$20600
(b) Net rental loss	$11300	$11300	$11300	$11300
(c) Taxable income (a – b)	$208700	$138700	$58700	$23700
(d) Marginal tax rate	47%	39%	32%	18%
(e) Tax benefit of negative gearing (b × d)	$5311	$4407	$3616	$2034
(f) Net cash outflow by investor (b – e)	$5989	$6893	$7684	$9266

Due to the progressive tax system in Australia, negative gearing is more beneficial to people in the higher income brackets who pay tax at the top marginal rate. But over the years, as tax brackets have changed and tax rates reduced, there are actually fewer people in the top tax bracket who can take full advantage of negative gearing benefits. In the above example, the taxpayer in the highest tax bracket (scenario 1) gets a tax refund of $5311. But if they were in the 18 per cent tax bracket (scenario 4), then they would only get $2034 back and be out of pocket by $9266. The worst scenario is where the other income is not sufficient to absorb the rental property loss. In this instance there is no tax refund, but the loss can be carried forward to following tax years.

♀ TIP

Don't let emotion take over when you are buying a house because there is too much at stake financially if you get too attached and go over your budget. You may end up with a property that is too highly negatively geared and struggle to meet the minimum repayments.

I am not a big fan of negative gearing as most people become asset rich but cash poor under this strategy. People who invest in several properties actually struggle to pay for them out of their cash flow. Negative gearing means that your expenses exceed your revenue so automatically your cash flow is negative. The tax benefit is still only a percentage of that loss.

> **⚠ PITFALL**
>
> Negative gearing strategy is not the be all and end all. When making an investment decision, make sure that you follow the 'ABC motto' — 'Absolute Bloody Cashflow!'
>
> While the example (on p. 90) shows different taxpayers getting nice refunds (ranging from $2034 to $5311), they are still out of pocket by the net cash outflow figure. The capital value of their properties must increase by at least that amount each year, otherwise they are falling further behind financially than they were at the start of the year.

The only situation in which you would negatively gear a property is when the capital growth of your property is greater than the negative cash outlay. Of course there are no guarantees that this is going to happen.

> **♀ TIP**
>
> A positively geared rental property, where the rent received is greater than your property expenses, provides a better financial result after tax than a negatively geared property. Of course you need to pay tax, but I would happily pay $5311 in tax if I knew that my bank account increased by $11300 without any effort!

33 INTEREST

If you take out a loan to purchase a rental property, you can claim the interest charged on that loan, or a portion of the interest, as a deduction. It is generally the biggest tax deduction for rental property investors.

> **🖐 TAX FACT**
>
> According to ATO statistics, interest claims represented more than 35.8 per cent of the total claims made by taxpayers for rental property deductions in the 2021–22 tax year.

While your property is rented, or available for rent, you may also claim interest charged on the loan you used to:

- finance renovations (such as adding a deck or second floor)
- purchase depreciating assets (such as an air-conditioner or stove)
- pay for repairs (such as roof repairs due to storm damage).

You can also claim interest on loans to purchase land on which to build a rental property. However, if your intention changes—for example, you decide to use the property for private purposes and you no longer use it to produce rent or other income—you cannot claim the interest.

You also cannot claim interest if you:

- start using the rental property for private purposes
- use a portion of the loan for private purposes (such as purchasing a new car or investing in a super fund)
- borrow against an existing rental property to buy a new home to live in.

✏ EXAMPLE

Joe and Mary decide to take out a $640 000 loan at 6.55 per cent. $590 000 is to be used to buy a rental property and $50 000 to buy a car.

$$\text{Interest for year 1} = \$640\,000 \times 6.55\% = \$41\,920$$

Apportionment of interest payment related to rental property:

Total interest expense × (rental property loan ÷ total borrowings) = deductible interest

$$\$41\,920 \times (\$590\,000 \div \$640\,000) = \$38\,645$$

Joe and Mary can each make an interest claim of $19 322 on their respective tax returns for the first year of the property.

Source: © Australian Taxation Office for the Commonwealth of Australia.

A common mistake is to claim a deduction for interest on the private portion of the loan. The interest expense must be apportioned between the 'deductible' and the 'private' portions of the total borrowings. The calculations can be complicated, particularly if you have a loan account that has a fluctuating balance due to a variety of deposits and withdrawals and it is used for both private purposes and rental property purposes.

If you use the equity on your existing property to buy a new house to live in, you cannot claim the interest on the additional borrowing even if you rent out the original house that the loan is secured against. Only the portion of the interest that relates to the original loan for the rental property will be deductible in this instance.

♀ TIP

If you expect your income to be lower next year (perhaps due to maternity leave or redundancy) you should consider prepaying a year's worth of interest in advance before 30 June this year. This strategy will bring forward deductions against the higher income and thus you'll get the tax benefit back at a higher marginal rate of tax.

♀ TIP

Don't overcommit when buying a property. Why do approximately 40 per cent of first home owners currently suffer mortgage stress? Because they purchased beyond their financial means. Make a budget before you buy. Lending organisations have been just as guilty in the past in giving too much. Just because they are willing to give you $1 million doesn't mean that you have to spend it all. A minimum 20 per cent deposit will create a buffer to cater for job losses, family planning and illness, interest rate rises and unexpected costs as well as avoid mortgage insurance. Never rely on a bonus to make regular repayments. It is better to buy a smaller house and live a comfortable life with regular family holidays than have a huge house and not be able to enjoy it because you work overtime and weekends.

34 DEPRECIATION AND LOW-VALUE POOLING

Depreciation

Behind interest, depreciation is usually the second-biggest deduction available for rental property investors, yet many don't claim it.

As your rental property gets older, the items within it experience wear and tear and they depreciate in value. The ATO allows property investors to claim a deduction for depreciation on:

- plant and equipment
- renovations or capital improvements commenced after 27 February 1992
- the building itself, if built after 18 July 1985 (and purchased before 9 May 2017 for previously used properties).

The amount of the depreciation claim can vary greatly depending on the age, use, fit-out and type of building. Plant and equipment items are basically items that can be 'easily' removed from the property as opposed to items that are permanently fixed to the structure of the building. These include things such as carpets, hot water systems, blinds and light fittings. They are usually written off over five to 10 years.

Due to the high deduction available for building costs, if you have bought an investment property that was not previously used before 9 May 2017 and it was built after 18 July 1985, it is definitely worthwhile organising a depreciation schedule from a quantity surveyor.

The ATO has a comprehensive list of more than 230 residential property items that can be depreciated.

⚠ PITFALL

Since 9 May 2017 a limit has been placed on depreciation deductions on residential rental properties to only those investors who actually purchased the plant and equipment. Subsequent owners will be unable to claim depreciation deductions on the written down value of assets purchased by previous owners.

The capital works allowance is a 2.5 per cent deduction available over 40 years, for the structural element of a building including fixed, irremovable assets. It is based on historical building costs excluding the cost of all 'plant' and non-eligible items and includes things such as the bricks and mortar, walls, flooring and wiring.

⚠ PITFALL

When you sell your rental property you will need to reduce your cost base, for CGT purposes, by the amount claimed for the building write-off allowance.

There are two methods that can be applied when depreciating property for tax purposes:

- prime cost (or straight line)
- diminishing value (or reducing balance).

Under the prime cost method the deduction for each year is calculated as a percentage of the cost as follows:

cost × days owned ÷ 365
× 100% plant's effective life (in years)

Under the diminishing value method the deduction is calculated as a percentage of the balance you have left to deduct:

opening undeducted cost × days owned
÷ 365 × 200%* plant's effective life (in years)

*Note: reduce to 150% if item purchased before 10 May 2006.

The ATO specifies the individual effective life for all plant and equipment items. If you claim using the diminishing value method, you are claiming a greater proportion of the asset's cost in the earlier years. If you claim using the prime cost method, you are claiming a lower but more constant portion of the available deductions over the lifetime of the property.

The intentions of the property investor will determine which method will be most suitable for them. My experience shows that most investors employ the diminishing value method, as depreciation deductions under this method are cumulatively higher over the first five years of ownership.

? FAQ

In April 2025 I bought a ten year old apartment to rent out. The previous owners gave me a copy of their depreciation schedule which includes various items such as carpet, a hot water system, the oven, air conditioner and lighting. I subsequently put in new curtains as well as an old clothes dryer and fridge from my house and bought a second hand TV from a mate. Can I claim depreciation on all of these items?

Since you bought the property after 9 May 2017, you cannot claim deductions for the decline in value of any existing depreciating assets in the apartment. Likewise you cannot claim deductions for the decline in value of the clothes dryer, refridgerator nor television as they are second-hand depreciating items. You can only claim the depreciation deductions for the curtains as they were new when installed.

Low-value pooling

In addition to using the diminishing value method, to maximise rental property deductions in the first five years, investors can 'pool' depreciable assets with written-down values less than $1000 and depreciate them at a more favourable 'pool rate' of 37.5 per cent.

♀ TIP

Provided they are not part of a set, you generally get an immediate deduction for depreciable assets costing $300 or less.

Once an asset is allocated to a low-value pool, it remains in the pool and it is not necessary to work out its adjustable value or decline in value separately. Only one annual calculation is required.

New assets acquired for less than $1000 during the year are allocated as 'low-cost assets' to the pool but the decline in value for these assets in the first year is at a rate of 18.75 per cent, or half the pool rate. Halving the rate recognises that assets may be allocated to the pool throughout the income year and eliminates the need to make separate calculations for each asset based on the date it was allocated to the pool. For subsequent years they are depreciated at the normal pool rate of 37.5 per cent.

The following example shows how to work out decline-in-value deductions.

✎ EXAMPLE

In the 2025–26 tax year, Rebecca allocated some depreciating assets she acquired in that year in relation to her rental property to a low-value pool, as shown in table 4.2.

TABLE 4.2: example of decline-in-value deduction calculations

	Cost or opening adjustable value	Low-value pool rate	Deduction for decline in value
Low-value assets:			
Various	$2679	37.5%	$1005
Low-cost assets acquired:			
Television (purchased 19/9/2025)	$687		
Microwave (purchased 31/3/2026)	$423		
Total low-cost assets acquired	$1110	18.75%	$208
Total deduction for decline in value for year ended 30 June 2026			$1213
Closing pool value at 30 June 2026			

$$= \text{Low-value assets} + \text{low-cost assets}$$
$$= (\$2679 - \$1005) + (\$1110 - \$208)$$
$$= \$2576, \text{ which will be depreciated}$$
$$\text{at 37.5 per cent in 2026–27 year}$$

Source: © Australian Taxation Office for the Commonwealth of Australia.

35 REPAIRS AND MAINTENANCE

Expenditure for repairs and maintenance is the tax deduction that confuses investors the most. Repairs generally involve a replacement or renewal of a worn–out or broken part and relate directly to wear and tear or other damage that occurred as a result of your renting out the property, such as:

- replacing part of the guttering or windows damaged in a storm
- replacing part of a fence damaged by a falling tree branch
- replacing broken windows
- repairing electrical appliances or machinery.

Maintenance is when work is done to prevent deterioration or fix existing deterioration including:

- painting a rental property
- oiling, brushing or cleaning something that is otherwise in good working condition
- maintaining plumbing.

This will generally be deductible if the property:

- continues to be rented on an ongoing basis
- remains available for rental but there is a short period when the property is unoccupied, such as when unseasonable weather causes cancellations of bookings or advertising is unsuccessful in attracting tenants.

If you no longer rent the property, the cost of repairs may still be deductible provided:

- the need for the repairs is related to the period in which the property was used to produce income
- you used the property to produce income during the year in which you incurred the cost of repairs.

You can't claim the total costs of repairs and maintenance in the year you paid for them if they did not relate directly to wear and tear or other damage that occurred due to renting out your property.

A common mistake is to claim initial repairs or capital improvements as immediate deductions. Initial repairs to rectify damage, defects or deterioration that existed at the time of purchasing a property are generally considered capital in nature and not deductible, even if you carried them out to make the property suitable for renting. However, these repairs may be claimed as capital works deductions over 40 years.

Capital improvements (such as landscaping, remodelling a bathroom or adding a deck) are non-deductible. This means you cannot claim the entire replacement cost you incurred in the year you incurred it. However, you may be able to claim the cost over a number of years as a capital works deduction or a deduction for decline in value. The cost of repairs to the property that amount to an improvement, and don't merely restore it back to its original condition, is generally capital and not deductible if it:

- provides something new
- furthers the income-producing ability or expected life of the property
- changes the character of the item you have improved
- goes beyond just restoring the efficient functioning of the property.

If you have to replace something identifiable as a separate item of capital equipment (such as a complete fence or building, a stove, kitchen cupboards or a refrigerator), you have not carried out a repair.

36 BORROWING AND LEGAL EXPENSES

Borrowing expenses

Borrowing expenses in relation to organising a loan to purchase a rental property are tax deductions. But you can't claim them all in the first year that they are incurred, unless they are $100 or less. If your total deductible expenses are more than $100, the deduction you claim for those expenses must be spread over five years or the term of the loan, whichever is less.

The types of borrowing expenses you can claim as income tax deductions include the following:

• costs for preparing and filing mortgage documents
• lender's mortgage insurance
• loan establishment fees
• mortgage broker fees

- stamp duty charged on your mortgage
- title search fees charged by your lender
- valuation fees required for loan approval.

Mortgage discharge expenses, including those ridiculously high penalty interest costs involved in discharging a fixed-rate mortgage, are deductible in the year they are incurred to the extent that you took out the mortgage as security for the repayment of money you borrowed to use to produce assessable income.

⚠ PITFALL

The following cannot be claimed as borrowing expenses:

- stamp duty charged by your state/territory government on the transfer (purchase) of the property title—this stamp duty can be included in calculating the 'cost base' of your property for CGT purposes
- insurance premiums where under the policy your loan will be paid out in the event that you die or become disabled or unemployed (this is a private expense)
- borrowing expenses on the portion of the loan you use for private purposes (for example, money used to buy a boat).

♀ TIP

Stamp duty, preparation and registration costs you incur on the lease of an Australian Capital Territory (ACT) property are deductible to the extent that you use the property as a rental property. This is because freehold title cannot be obtained for properties in the ACT. They are commonly acquired under a 99-year Crown lease.

✏ EXAMPLE

On 16 September 2025, Robert took out a 30-year loan of $450 000 to purchase a rental property. Robert's deductible expenses were:

- $950 stamp duty on the mortgage
- $650 loan establishment fees
- $250 valuation fees required for loan.

▶

Robert also paid $9200 stamp duty on the transfer of the property title, for which he cannot claim a tax deduction. However, this expense will form part of the 'cost base'.

Robert would work out the borrowing expense deduction for each year as follows:

Borrowing expenses × number of relevant days in year ÷ number of days in 5 years = deduction for year

2025–26 (288 days) = $1850 × 288 ÷ 1825 = $292

2026–27 (365 days) = $1850 × 365 ÷ 1825 = $370

2027–28 (366 days) = $1850 × 366 ÷ 1825 = $371

2028–29 (365 days) = $1850 × 365 ÷ 1825 = $370

2029–30 (365 days) = $1850 × 365 ÷ 1825 = $370

2030–31 (76 days) = $1850 x 76 ÷ 1825 = $77

Source: © Australian Taxation Office for the Commonwealth of Australia.

♀ TIP

If you repay your loan early and in fewer than five years, you can claim a deduction for the balance of the borrowing expenses in the year of repayment.

Legal expenses

Like borrowing expenses, some legal expenses associated with rental properties are deductible and some are capital in nature and not deductible.

The types of legal expenses you can claim as income tax deductions include:

- preparing a lease agreement with your tenant
- evicting a non-paying tenant.

Most legal expenses are not deductible as they are of a capital nature. These include costs:

- for the preparation of loan documents (can be claimed as borrowing expenses)
- for the purchase (or sale) of your property
- associated with resisting land resumption
- associated with defending your title to the property.

Non-deductible legal expenses that are capital in nature may form part of the cost base of your property for CGT purposes (for more information, see p. 108).

✏ EXAMPLE

Luke purchased a rental property for $810 000. The expenses Luke paid that he can claim as a deduction on his next tax return were:

- $350 solicitor's fees for preparation of the lease
- $950 solicitor's fees for preparation of loan documents
- $850 stamp duty on the mortgage.

The deductions for the $950 solicitor's fees for handling the loan documents and the $850 stamp duty on the mortgage are considered borrowing expenses and must be claimed over five years, or the term of the loan, whichever is shorter.

The legal expenses that Luke paid for that he cannot claim as a deduction (capital costs that may form part of the cost base of the property) were:

- $1125 solicitor's fees for purchase of the property
- $31185 stamp duty on the transfer of the property
- $60 title search fees.

Source: Australian Taxation Office.

37 OTHER RENTAL PROPERTY DEDUCTIONS

You may be entitled to claim an immediate deduction on these other property expenses in the income year you incur the expense:

- advertising for tenants
- bank charges
- body corporate fees and charges, also known as strata levies
- cleaning
- council rates
- electricity and gas
- gardening and lawnmowing
- in-house audio/video service charges
- insurance (building, contents and public liability)
- land tax
- letting fees
- pest control
- property agent's fees and commission
- quantity surveyor's fees
- secretarial and bookkeeping fees
- security patrol fees
- servicing costs—for example, servicing a water heater
- stationery and postage
- tax-related expenses
- telephone calls and rental
- water rates.

You can claim a deduction for these expenses only if you actually incur them and they are not paid by the tenant.

Land tax is a state tax imposed by each Australian state and territory (except the Northern Territory) and, as you might expect, each state has a different set of rules including different rates, thresholds and due dates. It is calculated on the unimproved value of the land (rather than the whole property value).

The tax is generally levied on the owners of land at midnight on 31 December of each year in New South Wales and Victoria (and 30 June for most other states) for land values greater than the threshold level, which are outlined in table 4.3. If you are liable for land tax you need to submit a land tax return. Owner-occupied homes or land used for primary production are generally exempt from land tax, while properties held in a trust or company generally have a zero threshold.

> **♀ TIP**
>
> While it may not be tax deductible, take out basic life insurance that will cover your mortgage so that you have peace of mind knowing that your loved ones are not forced to sell when you (and your income) are no longer around.

TABLE 4.3: state land tax thresholds

State	Land tax threshold	Website
ACT	$0	www.revenue.act.gov.au
NSW	$1 075 000	www.revenue.nsw.gov.au
Qld	$600 000	www.qld.gov.au
SA	$732 000	www.revenuesa.sa.gov.au
Tas.	$125 000	www.sro.tas.gov.au
Vic.	$50 000	www.sro.vic.gov.au
WA	$300 000	www.osr.wa.gov.au

You can claim a deduction for certain expenses you incur for the period your property is rented or is available for rent. However, you cannot claim expenses of a capital nature or private nature—although you may be able to claim decline-in-value deductions or capital works deductions for certain capital expenses or include certain capital costs in the cost base of the property for CGT purposes.

⚠ PITFALL

Expenses for which the ATO will not allow you to claim include:

- acquisition and disposal costs of the property
- body corporate payments to a special-purpose fund to pay for particular capital expenditure
- expenses you do not actually incur, such as water or electricity charges paid by your tenants
- expenses that are not related to the rental of a property, such as expenses connected to your own use of a holiday home that you rent out for part of the year
- travel in relation to inspecting, maintaining or collecting rent for a residential rental property.

♀ TIP

Make sure you have receipts to justify the deductions you are claiming, and can justify the connection between the expense and deriving the rental income (for example, it wasn't also for a private purpose).

38 FOREIGN INVESTMENT PROPERTIES

Australian tax residents have always been required to pay tax on their worldwide income. This includes declaring income earned from an overseas property that you may own in your Australian income tax return—even if it has been, or will be, taxed outside Australia.

If you have paid foreign tax in another country on that income, you may be entitled to an Australian foreign income tax offset, which provides relief from double taxation.

You can also claim the deductions (such as interest, repairs, depreciation, rates and insurance) as mentioned in tips 32–36 for a foreign rental property.

If your overseas property tax deductions are greater than your overseas rental income, you will have a foreign income loss. For many years, these foreign losses were quarantined and had to be carried forward to future years and only be offset against future foreign income.

However, many foreign property investors are not aware of the change in the rules a few years ago. Since 1 July 2008, foreign losses have not been quarantined from domestic income. This means that you can now 'negatively gear' your foreign income loss to reduce your Australian income.

⚠ PITFALL

An annual vacancy fee of at least $29 400 applies to foreign owners who leave their Australian properties unoccupied or not available for rent for 6 months or more each year. The fee increases for properties valued above $1 million. The fee is the same as the Foreign Investment Review Board's application fee for the purchase of an Australian property by a foreigner. It is paid via an annual return which can be found here www.ato.gov.au/FIRBvacancyfee/.

Before you calculate your net income, all foreign income, deductions and foreign tax paid must be converted to Australian dollars. There are two ways of doing this. Depending on your circumstances, you can use:

- the exchange rates prevailing at specific times (generally used for specific transactions such as monthly rent, asset purchases and one-off expenses such as rates and insurance)
- an average exchange rate (generally used for expenses incurred over a period such as loan interest).

> **⚠ PITFALL**
>
> Australian residents are generally taxed on any capital gains made on overseas property and must declare the gain in their income tax return. If the gain is taxable in Australia and you have paid foreign tax on it, you may be entitled to a foreign income tax offset.
>
> If an ATO audit detects that you did not declare offshore income there will be penalties and potentially a jail sentence if it was found to be an 'intentionally fraudulent act'.

> **⚠ PITFALL**
>
> From 1 April 2025 to 31 March 2027, foreign investors, including temporary residents and foreign-owned companies, cannot apply to buy existing homes in Australia unless an exception applies.

39 CAPITAL GAINS TAX

Careful tax planning is required by property investors when they intend to sell properties acquired after 19 September 1985, as the profit realised may be subject to capital gains tax (CGT). Capital gains are added to an individual's taxable income and taxed at their marginal tax rate.

> **♀ TIP**
>
> The simplest way to reduce CGT is to hold onto the investment for more than 12 months. Since 21 September 1999, investors have been entitled to claim a 50 per cent discount on capital gains they make on assets held for longer than a year. Since 8 May 2012, non-residents are no longer eligible for this discount on taxable Australian property.

> **⚠ PITFALL**
>
> Generally, an investment property owned for at least 12 months and then sold is entitled to 50 per cent discount on the capital gain. However, if your intention was to renovate and sell at a profit, rather than maintain the property as a long-term, income-producing investment, you may be taxed on the entire profit as a 'profit-making scheme'.

You will make a capital gain from the sale of your rental property to the extent that the capital proceeds you receive are more than the cost base of the property. The cost base of a property includes:

- the original purchase price
- incidental costs associated with acquiring the property—such as legal fees and stamp duty
- incidental costs associated with disposing of the property—such as legal fees and real estate agent's commissions
- improvements made to the property (less any depreciation previously claimed).

♀ TIP

If you are thinking of selling a profitable asset, such as shares or property, it may be worth deferring the sale exchange until after the end of the financial year. By doing so, you will get an extra year to pay any CGT liability and earn an extra year's interest until you eventually pay it.

CGT is payable in the year that you exchange, rather than the year that you settle, so make sure you exchange on a property after 1 July.

As discussed earlier, negative gearing is generally a good strategy for high-income earners as they get bigger refunds than lower income earners. Unfortunately it has the opposite effect when a property is sold and subject to CGT.

♀ TIP

A good strategy is to delay selling your investment property until a year when your income will be lower and you will fall into a lower marginal tax bracket. This is particularly relevant when investors are nearing retirement as they should consider delaying any CGT liability until they have retired and earn little or no income.

● TAX FACT

You can use your capital losses to offset the capital gains you make on other assets.

While a person's principal place of residence is CGT-free when they sell it, it is possible to move out of the property, rent it and still claim this exemption for up to six years. After that time, the CGT clock is no longer frozen and starts ticking.

⚠ PITFALL

Although there is generally no GST on residential properties, if you are buying new residential premises (or potential residential land), you may need to pay GST at settlement. The purchaser will pay the withheld amount of GST direct to the ATO with the balance of the sale price of the property, minus the GST withholding amount and other settlement adjustments, to the vendor. For more information visit www.ato.gov.au/GSTatsettlement

🎁 BONUS RESOURCES

For more information about CGT, the ATO has the excellent *Personal investors guide to capital gains tax* (NAT 4152).

⚠ PITFALL

Since 1 July 2020, foreign residents who own houses that they previously lived in whilst they were in Australia cannot claim the main residence CGT exemption when they subsequently sell. This means that a hefty capital gains tax bill accrues from the time the owner purchased their home, rather than the point at which they moved overseas (plus up to a further six years that they rented the place after being their home).

? FAQ

If we move into the granny flat in the back of our property and rent out the main house, are we subject to capital gains tax?

When you move into your granny flat, it will be treated as a separate asset for CGT purposes. You will need to consider on which asset to claim the principal place of residence exemption — ideally the property with the greatest opportunity for growth, which will probably be the main house. Of course, any periods that you live in both places at the same time are exempt from CGT.

There is a CGT exemption for granny flat arrangements where there is a formal written agreement in place. Under the measure, CGT will not apply to the creation, variation or termination of a formal written granny flat arrangement. This will remove the adverse tax consequences for the property owner while providing protection for older parents or people with disabilities. The CGT exemption will not be available for a property that is not the principal home of the taxpayer (for example, a rental property that happens to contain a granny flat).

Investment properties that are supplied for low to moderate income tenants for at least three years via Community Housing Providers (CHP) as affordable housing will be eligible for an additional 10 per cent CGT discount. This will effectively increase the CGT discount up to a maximum of 60 per cent. To be eligible, rent must be charged at a discount below the private market rental rate as determined by the registered CHP, consistent with state and territory affordable housing policies.

40 PAYG WITHHOLDING VARIATION

As mentioned earlier, one of the major downsides to negative gearing is cash flow.

My preference is that you wait until the end of the year to get your refund as it is a forced form of saving. But if cash flow is tight, you may want to complete a pay-as-you-go (PAYG) withholding variation application, which reduces the tax from your monthly pay. The form is virtually a mini tax return which estimates your taxable income. You still need to lodge an annual tax return.

✎ EXAMPLE

Jason is on the highest marginal tax rate. In the year ending 30 June 2026 he expects to incur a net rental loss of $20 000. Instead of waiting to lodge his 2025–26 tax return in July 2026 and getting a refund of $9400, he can submit a PAYG withholding variation application with the ATO in May 2025. As a result, Jason has $783.33 less PAYG tax withheld from his salary each month to help him meet his mortgage commitments instead of waiting until the end of the financial year.

♀ TIP

The rate of withholding will hopefully match your year-end tax liability. If you underestimate your income then expect to have a tax shortfall, which isn't desirable. Instead, make sure you give yourself a buffer by not being too aggressive with estimating deductions.

If your circumstances change after your PAYG variation is approved (perhaps you increased the rent, your expenses are lower than expected or you sold your property), then submit a new PAYG variation straight away. Otherwise you may have an unwanted tax liability at the end of the year.

You can lodge your application in paper form or electronically over the internet. The varied rate of withholding will start from the next payday after your pay office receives the notice of withholding variation approval from the ATO.

◖ TAX FACT

PAYG withholding variations are not solely available to taxpayers who are negatively gearing rental properties. They can also be used for other purposes where a taxpayer's assessable income is substantially reduced for tax-deductible expenditure such as work-related car expenses, self-education costs or margin-loan interest.

Your variation generally finishes on 30 June each year so you need to do a new PAYG withholding variation application each year—they do not roll forward. To continue to have reduced tax withheld after this date, you must lodge another PAYG withholding variation application at least six weeks beforehand; that is, by 15 May each year.

41 CO-OWNERSHIP OF YOUR INVESTMENT PROPERTY

It may seem simple but the way that rental income and expenses are divided between co-owners varies depending on whether the co-owners are joint tenants or tenants in common or there is a partnership carrying on a rental property business.

Most rental activities are a form of investment and do not amount to carrying on a business. However, where you are carrying on a rental property business in partnership with others, you must divide the net rental income or loss according to your partnership agreement. You must do this whether the legal interests in the rental properties are different to the partners' entitlements to profits and losses under the partnership agreement. If you do not have a partnership agreement, you should divide your net rental income or loss between the partners equally.

To determine whether a property portfolio amongst partners is carried as a rental property business rather than mere investors, the ATO considers:

- the significant size and scale of the rental property activities

- the number of hours spent on the activities

- the extensive personal involvement in the activities, and

- the business-like way the activities are planned, organised and carried on.

💡 TIP

If your rental property activities amount to a partnership carrying a business, then you may be eligible for the generous small business concessions discussed in more detail in Part VII.

Co-owners who are not carrying on a rental property business are simply regarded as investors and must divide the income and expenses for the rental property in line with their legal interest in the property. If they own the property as joint tenants then they each hold an equal interest in the property, with equal rights and obligations. When one of the owners in a joint tenancy dies, that owner's interest in the property passes direct to the survivors without the property having to go through the courts.

💡 TIP

Interest on any monies borrowed by only one of the co-owners which is exclusively used to acquire that person's interest in the investment property does not need to be divided between all of the co-owners irrespective of what their legal interests in the property are.

If the co-owners own the investment property as tenants in common, they may hold unequal interests in the property. For example, one may hold a 25 per cent interest and the other the remaining 75 per cent interest. Rental income and expenses must be attributed to each co-owner according to their legal interest in the property, despite any agreement between co-owners, either oral or in writing, stating otherwise. If you are unsure about whether you hold your legal interest as a joint tenant or a tenant in common, read the title deed for the rental property.

⚠ PITFALL

Unlike joint tenancy, when a tenant in common dies, the property passes to that tenant's estate where they have the right to leave their share of the property to any beneficiary as a portion of their estate.

☛ TAX FACT

If you had any shares in joint names, you are not required to lodge a separate partnership tax return. Simply show your proportion of any dividends paid in your individual tax return.

? FAQ

Can I claim all the interest on an investment property that I own with my wife as I am earning $200 000 (that is, on the highest marginal tax rate) but she is at home with the kids and doesn't earn any other income?

Nice try but unfortunately not. Any expenses for joint properties need to be apportioned to each owner based on your respective percentages of ownership. The upside is that when you sell the property and must pay CGT down the track, your wife (assuming her income levels are still low) will not have to pay as much for her share of any gain.

42 BUILD-TO-RENT PROPERTIES

It seems that every time that I turn on the TV these days there is another story about the rental shortage crisis hitting the major cities across the country. So it is good to see that the Federal and State Government authorities are providing a raft of incentives for property developers to build specific 'build-to-rent' (BTR) properties to increase the supply of affordable housing and attempt to reduce the stress on tenants.

Somewhat different to the 'build-to-own' concept that we are accustomed to in Australia, BTR developments are quite popular in both the US and UK. They are apartment complexes that are designed, constructed, owned and ultimately managed by a property developer, who then rents them out to tenants.

In 2008, the Federal Government—in partnership with the State Governments — introduced the National Rental Affordability Scheme (NRAS) to encourage large-scale investment in affordable housing with annual incentives for up to 10 years to approved participants who rent dwellings to approved people on low to moderate incomes at a rate of at least 20 per cent below market rent. However, the NRAS is expected to end in 2026 with the government coming up with alternative incentives.

With the cost to develop BTR properties being quite high, the sector will see mostly large property developers, institutional investors, large global investors, sovereign wealth funds and pension funds as well as local superannuation funds. For the investment proposal to be attractive to these investors, the governments throughout the country are offering a number of incentives to reduce the costs of holding.

● TAX FACT

To encourage greater incentives for foreign investors to be involved in residential BTR projects in Australia, the 2023–24 federal budget reduced the withholding rate for eligible fund payments from managed investment trusts (MIT) attributable to BTR projects from 30 per cent to 15 per cent.

● TAX FACT

The capital works allowance is 4 per cent for eligible build-to-rent projects.

At a State level, Governments are enticing property developers to commence BTR projects with usually a minimum requirement of there being at least 50 self-contained dwellings used specifically for BTR purposes and being owned and managed by the same owner. Most States offer a 50 per cent land tax incentive although Tasmania will increase its land tax concession to 100 per cent if the BTR developments are rented at 20 per cent below market rate.

● TAX FACT

In NSW there is a 50 per cent land tax discount for new BTR housing projects until 2040 as well as an exemption from foreign investor duty and land tax surcharges.

In both Tasmania and Victoria, there is a 50 per cent reduction on the taxable value of the land used for a BTR development for up to 30 years. In Victoria there is also an exemption from any absentee owner surcharge in respect of that land during that time.

In Queensland, there is a 50 per cent reduction on the taxable value of the land used for a BTR development for up to 20 years as well as an exemption from foreign acquirer duty and land tax foreign surcharge.

In South Australia, there is a 50 per cent reduction on the taxable value of the land until 2040.

In Western Australia, there is a 50 per land tax exception for up to 20 years for developments built prior to July 2032.

▲ PITFALL

Aside from providing more stock in the rental marketplace, BTR developments offer a number of benefits to tenants including lower bonds and the stability of a long-term lease without fear of the owner selling up. However, the rents are usually higher (due to more amenities/facilities along with a dedicated manager) and the properties remain in the hands of developers, meaning those aspiring to own their own home one day may struggle due to no new stock available. There may also be issues with no body corporate to oversee the long-term maintenance of the exterior of properties along with complaints about tenant or visitors' behaviour.

PART V
YOUR SHARES

Owning shares can bring about some important tax considerations for shareholders.

> **🖤 TAX FACT**
>
> According to an Australian Investor study by the Australian Securities Exchange (ASX) in June 2023, 38 per cent of the population, owned shares directly, with 51 per cent holding investments in addition to their home and super fund. The study also found that 22 per cent of share owners began investing in the last two years.

Share ownership in Australia increased substantially in the 1990s following the privatisation of a number of government-owned enterprises (such as Telstra and the Commonwealth Bank) and the demutualisation of many financial service providers (such as AMP, MBF, NRMA and NIB) before the GFC (2008) and the COVID-19 pandemic (2020–22) shook investor confidence.

For the majority of Australians the complexity of tax returns increased substantially as a result, with the advent of dividends, franking credits, share buybacks, rights issues, margin loans, capital gains tax and the like.

> **🖤 TAX FACT**
>
> If you hold shares, the ATO requires you to keep proper records for tax purposes, including:
>
> - 'buy' and 'sell' contracts for five years from the date you dispose of your shares
> - dividend statements for five years from the date you lodge your tax return.

In part V, I will focus on the tax implications of owning a share portfolio as well as looking at ways to minimise any CGT liability in the future.

🛈 BONUS RESOURCES

For more information about tax and shares, the ATO has an excellent publication called *You and your shares 2025* (NAT 2632).

43 DIVIDENDS

Being a shareholder entitles you to a share of a company's profits that are usually paid as dividends. In Australia, there are two types of dividends that are assessable for tax purposes:

- franked dividends
- unfranked dividends.

⚠ PITFALL

According to the ATO, if a private company lends money to a shareholder (or associate) and the loan is not fully repaid before the end of the income year, the outstanding amount may be treated as a non-commercial loan and assessed as an unfranked dividend in the shareholder's tax return to the extent of the private company's retained earnings.

Franked dividends are dividends paid by Australian companies from profits that have been taxed previously. A dividend which carries tax credits for the whole dividend is known as a fully franked dividend.

Unfranked dividends are dividends paid by Australian companies from profits that have not had any company tax paid on them.

♀ TIP

Bank charges and any interest payments on funds borrowed to acquire shares are generally tax deductible.

✋ TAX FACT

Franked dividends paid to non-resident individuals are exempt from Australian income tax. However, they are not entitled to any franking tax offset for franked dividends.

Any unfranked dividends paid to a non-resident are subject to a final withholding tax, generally 15 per cent if Australia has a double taxation agreement with the taxpayer's resident country, otherwise at 30 per cent.

When an Australian company pays you a dividend, it must also send you a statement advising:

- the amount of the dividend that is unfranked
- the amount of the dividend that is franked
- any franking credits
- any TFN withholding tax withheld on unfranked dividends.

♀ TIP

Make sure you quote your TFN to any company that pays you a dividend, otherwise withholding tax at the highest marginal rate (47 per cent) will be deducted on any unfranked dividends paid to you. If you have TFN tax withheld you must include it in your tax return so that you receive the credit in your assessment.

This is an example of what a dividend statement would look like:

ABC Limited

ABN 12 345 678 901

Shareholder dividend statement

Payment date 15 February 2026

Notification of 2025 final dividend — paid 15 February 2026

Security description	No. of shares	Unfranked amount	Franked amount	Franking credit
Ordinary shares	18 000	$500	$700	$300
TFN amount	$0.00			
Net dividend	$1200.00			

Please note that your tax file number has been received and recorded.

Please retain this advice for taxation purposes.

Please advise promptly in writing of any change of address.

Source: © Australian Taxation Office for the Commonwealth of Australia.

♀ TIP

Taxpayers regularly get the timing of the dividend payments wrong. Only dividends paid between 1 July and 30 June the following year should be included in your return. Confusion usually occurs when a final dividend is paid in July or August yet the dividend statement says that it is in respect of the year ended 30 June. In this instance the dividend should be declared in the following tax year.

☝ TAX FACT

If you had any shares in joint names, you are not required to lodge a separate partnership tax return. Simply show your proportion of any dividends paid in your individual tax return.

Franking credits

Franking credits, also known as imputation credits, were introduced in 1985 to prevent the double taxation of dividends to individual shareholders after companies had already paid tax on the profits distributed.

Franking credits are amounts of tax paid by the company that are allocated to your franked dividend. There is no franking credit associated with an unfranked dividend.

> **⬥ TAX FACT**
>
> Dividends paid to shareholders by Australian companies are taxed under an 'imputation' system where tax paid by a company may be imputed to shareholders. Any tax paid by the company is allocated by way of franking credits attached to the dividends paid to shareholders.

The amount of the franking credit is calculated as follows:

$$\text{Franking credit} = \text{franked dividend paid} \times \text{company tax rate} \div (100\% - \text{company tax rate})$$

The company tax rate for businesses with turnover greater than $50 million is 30 per cent, but reduces to 25 per cent for small/medium companies under this threshold. So if you receive a dividend from a public company, you calculate the franking credit as follows:

$$\text{Franking credit} = \text{franked dividend} \times 30 \div 70$$

> **✎ EXAMPLE**
>
> On 15 February 2026 an Australian resident company, ABC Ltd, paid Peter, a resident individual, a fully franked dividend of $700 and an unfranked dividend of $500.
>
> Peter's assessable income for 2025–26 in respect of the dividend is:
>
> | | |
> |---|---|
> | Unfranked dividend | $500 |
> | Franked dividend | $700 |
> | Franking credit ($700 × 30 ÷ 70) | $300 |
> | **Total assessable dividends** | **$1500** |

The franking credit is included in the definition of assessable income and must also be declared in your income tax return. Tax is payable at your applicable tax rate on these amounts but the franking credit becomes a tax offset against any tax payable.

Apart from disclosing it as income, there is no requirement to claim the tax offset in your tax return. The ATO will automatically put it on your notice of assessment. The offset can be used to reduce any liability from all forms of income and from net taxable capital gains.

✎ EXAMPLE

Using the dividend from the previous example, Peter's tax payable following the dividend is calculated as follows:

Total assessable dividends	$1500
Other assessable income	$78 500
Taxable income	**$80 000**
Tax on taxable income	$14 788
Add: Medicare levy (2%)	$1600
Less: Franking tax offset	($300)
Net tax payable	**$16 088**

Individuals who have franking credits greater than any tax payable do not lose them but get them refunded instead.

Dividend reinvestment plans

Not all dividends are paid in cash. If it is a private company they can be credited against the shareholder's loan account. Or you can be issued with new shares in lieu of the dividend via a 'dividend reinvestment plan' (DRP) or scheme.

Any dividend used to acquire shares under the DRP forms part of your Australian taxable income and you are required to pay tax on these reinvested dividends.

You are also subject to tax on any capital gain made when you dispose of shares you have received under a DRP. For the purpose of calculating any capital gain or loss, the cost of the shares acquired under a DRP is taken as the market price on the date of the dividend as shown on the statement.

44 SHARES OWNED BY LOW INCOME EARNERS

There can be some significant benefits in holding shares in the name of the spouse who is on the lower income, because any dividends (and capital gains) are taxed at a lower rate.

The marginal income tax rates for resident individuals for the 2025–26 financial year are shown in table 5.1.

TABLE 5.1: tax rates for individuals excluding levies (2025–26)

Taxable income	Tax on this income
0–$18 200	Nil
$18 201–$45 000	16c for each $1 over $18 200
$45 001–$135 000	$4288 plus 30c for each $1 over $45 000
$135 001–$190 000	$31 288 plus 37c for each $1 over $135 000
$190 001 and over	$51 638 plus 45c for each $1 over $190 000

Source: © Australian Taxation Office for the Commonwealth of Australia.

♀ TIP

For those earning less than $135 000, franked dividends are almost tax-free because they get a credit for the 30 per cent company tax already paid—the same as the marginal rate at that level.

For those on lower marginal tax rates (that is, earning less than $45 000), the excess franking tax offsets can be used to reduce your tax liability from other forms of income, including net taxable capital gains, or can even be refunded.

✎ EXAMPLE

Tom earns $310 000 while his wife Suzie earns $20 000. They just sold their house and are considering purchasing a share portfolio of stocks in blue-chip companies. As Suzie has a marginal tax rate of 18 per cent (including the 2 per cent Medicare levy), it is more beneficial for her to own the portfolio in her name than for Tom to own it, as he is in the highest tax bracket of 47 per cent.

The tax savings on a share portfolio in Suzie's name that generates an annual income stream of franked dividends of, say, $20 000 would be as much as $7098, or 35.49 per cent of the income received.

⚠ PITFALL

A share portfolio in the low-income-earning spouse's name may have an impact on any government benefits being received, as dividend income and capital gains are included under the income test and the share portfolio itself is assessed by Centrelink under its assets test.

If there are some significant capital gains in a portfolio, then they may push the low-income earner into a higher tax bracket, thus negating some of the tax benefits that may be received. In this instance it may be an idea to spread the disposal over a few income years.

There is also a need to look into a crystal ball and forecast what income levels will be for spouses in future years, especially if the current income is abnormally low, and that events such as returning to work after the kids go back to school are fully considered prior to making any purchase.

✐ EXAMPLE

If, in two years' time, Suzie gets a full-time job with a salary of $190 000 and Tom decides to reduce the number of days he works and only earns $60 000 per annum, there is no longer any benefit in having the share portfolio in Suzie's name as she is now in a high tax bracket of 47 per cent while Tom only pays 34.5 per cent.

While it is possible to transfer shares across to the other partner's name in an off-market transfer, such an event would trigger CGT, which might negate any benefit gained by such a switch.

♀ TIP

Senior Australians are not required to pay any income tax if their income is below $32 279 for singles (or $28 974 each if a couple). As a result, notwithstanding the risks associated with share-price fluctuations, an investment strategy of having a share portfolio that generates fully franked dividends (and franking credits subsequently refunded) may be quite lucrative for those eligible for the senior and pensioner tax offset.

---

45 BORROWING TO BUY SHARES

A common, yet risky, investment strategy used by share investors has been to borrow money, usually via a margin loan, to buy shares.

⚠ PITFALL

Borrowing is a good strategy in a rising market, but it can multiply any losses in a falling market. The last thing you want is a loan to repay but no shares to show for it. Don't consider borrowing if you are new to investing.

Just like the tax rules for investment properties, if you borrow money to buy a share portfolio, you can claim a tax deduction for the loan interest, provided it is reasonable to expect that assessable income (dividends or capital gains) will be derived from the share investment. If the loan has a private component, you will only be able to claim interest incurred on the part of the loan used to acquire the shares.

The benefit of such a strategy is that the interest expense should offset any dividend income received, resulting in franking credits that can be offset against other taxable income. Hopefully the shares increase in value under this strategy and any capital gains are only realised in a later year when the taxpayer is on a lower tax rate, for example, in retirement.

♀ TIP

If you expect to earn a lower income next tax year (for example, due to redundancy or maternity leave), an excellent strategy to consider is prepaying interest 12 months in advance before year end on your margin loan to maximise your tax deduction based on the higher marginal tax rate.

Borrowing expenses (such as establishment fees, legal expenses and stamp duty on loans) may be claimed for tax purposes. If borrowing expenses are more than $100, then they must be apportioned over five years or over the term of the loan, whichever is less. Borrowing expenses under $100 are fully deductible in the year incurred.

⚠ PITFALL

For a borrowing strategy to work you need to get a return greater than the cost of the interest rate that you are paying (which is generally at a premium for margin loans), otherwise you are falling further behind despite receiving the tax benefits. Remember the ABC motto: Absolute Bloody Cashflow!

Some investors use a capital-protected borrowings strategy, where shares are bought using a borrowing arrangement where the borrower is wholly or partly protected against a fall in the market value of the investments.

☝ TAX FACT

Any interest paid for capital protection under a capital-protected borrowing arrangement for shares is not deductible but instead is treated as if it were a payment for a put option.

⚠ PITFALL

While there was a change in the law in September 2007 that made it possible to borrow within self managed super funds, special rules apply. Seek professional advice on how to structure this to avoid any contravention of the complex superannuation rules.

? FAQ

Is it possible to claim the interest charged on money borrowed to purchase shares when there were no dividends paid in that tax year?

Yes, most definitely. So long as it is reasonable to expect some assessable income from this share investment over time, be it dividends or capital gains, then you can claim a deduction for loan interest in the tax year in which it is incurred, whether or not you receive income in the same year.

46 OTHER SHARE DEDUCTIONS

The following are examples of deductions that you may be able to claim for costs incurred in deriving income from shares.

Ongoing management fees

Ongoing management fees are allowable deductions, but only a proportion of the fee is deductible if the advice covers non-investment matters or is related to investments that do not produce assessable income.

> **⚠ PITFALL**
>
> Any cost for drawing up an initial investment plan is not tax-deductible.

Travel expenses

Travel expenses incurred to visit a stockbroker or annual general meeting are fully tax-deductible to the extent that the sole purpose of the travel relates to the share investment. If the travel is predominantly of a private nature, such as a holiday, only the expenses that relate directly to servicing your portfolio will be allowable as a tax deduction.

Journals and publications

Specialist investment journals and publications, subscriptions or sharemarket information services you use to manage your share portfolio can be claimed against your investment income.

Internet access

If you use the internet to manage your portfolio—such as buying and selling shares online—the cost of internet access will be deductible to the extent that the internet is used for this purpose. Any private usage is not claimable and must be added back.

Other deductions

Any other expenses you incur that relate directly to maintaining your portfolio are also deductible, including:

- bookkeeping expenses
- telephone
- postage.

47 CAPITAL GAINS TAX ON SHARES

With a potential to go up to 47 per cent, CGT can have a hugely negative impact when calculating the net return on an investment. It is a tax imposed upon gains made from the disposal of assets, usually shares or investment properties, that were acquired after 19 September 1985. When a net capital gain arises it is included in your taxable income and is subject to income tax at the marginal tax rates.

You make a capital gain or loss when a 'CGT event' occurs. These events could be when you:

- sell your shares
- have your shares redeemed, cancelled, surrendered or considered valueless by a liquidator
- receive a payment (other than dividends) from a company as a shareholder
- give away your shares.

The capital gain is calculated on the difference between the proceeds that you receive from the sale of your shares and the amount you originally paid for them. Brokerage is included in your cost base.

♀ TIP

The simplest way to reduce CGT is to hold onto the investment for more than 12 months. Since September 1999, a 50 per cent discount on capital gains is allowed for shares held for longer than a year.

⚠ PITFALL

If you do try to wait for the 12 months' holding period to tick over, be careful that the sharemarket doesn't collapse during this time. A dramatic fall in share price could erase any tax benefit that the 50 per cent discount provides if you are not careful.

Shares sold back to a company under a buyback arrangement result in a capital gain or loss. Part of the buyback price may be treated as an assessable dividend for income tax purposes. If the buyback comes from a listed company, a class ruling is usually issued to assist shareholders with any tax implications.

To calculate any capital gain, the ATO requires you to keep proper records for tax purposes including:

- 'buy' and 'sell' contract notes, showing the date and amounts
- dividend statements for any dividend reinvestment schemes that you participated in.

The ATO will allow you to establish a CGT asset register (but only if it is in a certain format) if you do not want to keep your records, particularly if you hold shares for a long time. For more information, see the ATO's Taxation Ruling TR 2002/10 Income tax: capital gains tax: asset register.

💡 TIP

Since 1 July 2016, investment in a qualifying early stage innovation company (ESIC) by sophisticated investors, may result in a number of tax incentives including:

- 20 per cent non-refundable carry forward tax offset on the amount paid for the investment, capped at $200 000 per annum
- no tax on capital gains realised on qualifying shares in an ESIC held between 12 months and less than ten years.

The incentives are not available to those who are not sophisticated investors and whose total investment in an income year is more than $50 000.

🎁 BONUS RESOURCES

For more information about CGT, the ATO has the excellent *Personal investors guide to capital gains tax* (NAT 4152).

48 REALISING CAPITAL LOSSES

One of the best ways to reduce your CGT bill is to offset any gains that you have made during the financial year with any losses incurred on other share investments. It is important to note that the losses must be crystallised (or realised) in order for them to be offset against any capital gains made. If a loss remains unrealised (not sold) at the end of the financial year, you cannot claim it in your return until the year that you actually dispose of the investment.

✐ EXAMPLE

Peter makes a $6200 capital gain on the sale of BHP shares in July 2025. He also owns shares in another stock, XYZ, which he bought for $10 000 but which are now only worth $4000. If he realises this loss by selling these shares before 30 June 2026 he can reduce his taxable capital gain by $6000 to only $200. If Peter disposes of these XYZ shares after 1 July 2026, then he must pay tax on the whole $6200 gain.

It is good tax-planning practice to see if there is an opportunity to reduce the tax on gains made earlier in the year by selling a few non-performing shares. This is particularly relevant if the sharemarket is performing like a roller-coaster and there is a slump after a big rise earlier in the year.

♀ TIP

Maintain an Excel spreadsheet to keep track of the cost base and market value of your share portfolio on a stock-by-stock basis. This will assist with the tax-planning process to help determine which stocks could be sold to offset capital gains already made during the year.

Obviously, if you haven't made any gains in the year then there is no need to crystallise any losses that you are currently carrying in your share portfolio.

♀ TIP

Realised capital losses can be carried forward indefinitely until they are fully utilised. Check your past tax returns for any available from previous years.

While you could purchase back your shares that have been realised for the loss, it is not advisable. Although yet to be challenged in the courts, the ATO has warned that the practice of 'wash sales' (where you sell shares and buy them back straight away for the purposes of realising capital losses to offset against other capital gains) could be considered an avoidance of income tax under Part IVA of the tax legislation. This comes with some hefty tax penalties.

If you are considering such a scenario, ensure that you purchase a different number of shares from the number that you originally sold. Or if your portfolio simply needs to be rebalanced in a particular industry, then buy a similar stock instead. For example, if you sell your Westpac Bank shares to crystallise a capital loss, buy a different bank stock such as ANZ or Commonwealth Bank instead as a replacement.

Also note that capital losses must be applied against capital gains prior to any 50 per cent discount being applied to shares held for more than 12 months.

✎ EXAMPLE

Natalie has a $500 discounted capital gain based on a raw capital gain of $1000 from ABC shares held more than 12 months. She also incurred a $700 capital loss from the disposal of XYZ shares. She must offset the capital loss of $700 against the $1000 raw capital gain, before applying the 50 per cent discount on the remaining $300 gain. As a result she will need to pay tax on the $150 discounted net capital gain.

---

49 INHERITING SHARE PORTFOLIOS

If you receive shares from a deceased estate you need to be aware of some consequences for tax. Future dividends received are treated as normal income. The only variation is if a child under 18 receives income via a testamentary trust—then it is taxed at adult rates instead of the high rates imposed on minors.

While normal CGT rules apply if a beneficiary sells an asset they have inherited, there are a few variances depending on when they inherited the shares and when they were originally purchased by the deceased.

All inherited shares are considered to have been acquired for CGT purposes on the day that the person died. If that was before 20 September 1985, you disregard any capital gain or loss made from the asset.

If the shares were originally acquired before 20 September 1985, your cost base is the market value of the asset on the day the person died.

⚠ PITFALL

According to the ATO, if the shares were originally acquired by the deceased before 20 September 1985, you must use the market value on the day the person died, not the market value on the day you received the shares.

👍 TAX FACT

While death can be sudden, it may be possible to do some tax planning before someone dies:

- Use any capital losses that are accumulated or unrealised prior to death, as these cannot be passed on to beneficiaries.
- Bequeath share portfolios to beneficiaries on lower taxable incomes so that tax paid on income and capital gains in the future are minimal and the capital is preserved for as long as possible.
- If the estate is substantial and there are children under age 18 who are potential beneficiaries, consider establishing a testamentary trust so they can access the favourable adult marginal tax rates.

If a deceased person acquired their shares on or after 20 September 1985, your cost base is taken to be the deceased person's cost base of the shares on the day the person died. The indexation method can be used for capital gains purposes if the deceased person died before 21 September 1999.

50 SHARE TRADERS VERSUS SHARE INVESTORS

The distinction between share traders and share investors is significant for tax purposes as you deal with gains and losses differently.

The ATO will consider you to be a share trader if you conduct your business activities for the sole purpose of earning income from the buying and selling of shares. Losses incurred are treated the same as any other losses from business—provided the non-commercial losses rules are satisfied, an immediate deduction is available against other taxable income.

> **👍 TAX FACT**
>
> In financial years when shares plummet, it is quite common for taxpayers to try to class themselves as share traders.

> **👍 TAX FACT**
>
> To be classed as a share trader, the ATO may ask you to prove you are carrying on a share trading business, including providing evidence that shows:
>
> • the purchase and sale of shares on a regular basis
> • the use of any share trading techniques

- decisions based on thorough analysis of relevant market information
- a contingency plan in the event of a major market shift
- a trading plan showing analysis and research of each potential investment and the market, and any formula for deciding when to hold or sell investments.

The ATO will consider you to be a share investor if you:

- invest in shares with the sole intention of earning income from dividends and capital growth
- are eligible for the 50 per cent CGT discount on gain
- claim losses incurred as a capital loss and not as an immediate deduction
- carry forward capital losses to be offset against future capital gains.

👍 TAX FACT

In financial years when shares rocket up, it is quite common for taxpayers to try to class themselves as share investors so they can get the 50 per cent CGT discount on gains made for shares held for more than 12 months.

How you treat your investment activities in prior tax returns is the main factor in determining the correct way to deal with losses in the current tax year. If there has been little or no change in your investment activity, you should treat the investments in the same manner again in the current year.

✏ EXAMPLE

George has been purchasing shares for a number of years for the purpose of earning income from dividends. In a previous year George sold shares and claimed the 50 per cent CGT discount. It is expected that George will claim any losses in the current year as capital losses.

If you change from being a share investor to being a share trader (or vice versa) the ATO may request evidence that proves the change is accurate and that you have not declared your income incorrectly in previous tax returns.

> **⚠ PITFALL**
>
> The ATO has issued a warning to taxpayers who seek to change their status from that of a share investor to a share trader. For more information, see *Taxpayer Alert 2009/12*.
>
> If an ATO audit finds that you have incorrectly claimed trading losses and you are unable to satisfactorily show that you are carrying on an investment business, your deduction will be disallowed and penalties may apply.

51 RIGHTS AND OPTIONS

Companies sometimes issue their shareholders with rights or options to purchase additional shares.

A 'one-for-ten' rights issue means that shareholders are entitled to purchase an additional share for every 10 shares that they own. The right can be exercised, sold on the stock exchange or simply allowed to lapse.

> **👍 TAX FACT**
>
> If you receive rights, the ATO will not require you to include them in your assessable income provided:
>
> * you already own shares in the company and the rights were issued to you because of this ownership
> * your shares, and the rights, were not traditional securities or convertible interests, or were being treated as revenue assets or trading stock at the time they were issued
> * the rights were not acquired under an employee share scheme.

Where the above criteria are satisfied then the only tax consequences that may arise with rights issues involve CGT. In other situations, rights issues may result in having to disclose assessable income in your tax return.

If you are issued a right to sell your shares (that is, a put), then the market value of the right should be included in your assessable income at the time of issue and will form part of your cost base for the rights or shares, if you exercised the rights.

Companies may also issue their shareholders with options. If you receive an option, you have the right to acquire or sell shares in the company at a specified price on a specified date. These options can be traded on the stock exchange or allowed to lapse.

👍 TAX FACT

Options are similar to rights except that they are normally held for a longer period than rights before they lapse or must be exercised. According to the ATO, options can be issued to both existing shareholders and non-shareholders while rights can only be issued initially to existing shareholders.

Exchange-traded options are types of options that are not created by the company but by independent third parties and are traded on the stock exchange. Option trading will generally be considered a business activity and subject to the normal business income rules.

⚠ PITFALL

Option trading is the quickest way to make money, but it is also the quickest way to lose money. I have seen more people lose money on options than make money on them.

52 EMPLOYEE SHARE SCHEMES

Some companies give employees the chance to participate in employee share schemes (ESS) by offering ESS interests such as shares, rights or options to be acquired at a discount, which are then subject to tax. ESS interests can be taxed under the employee share scheme rules as well as being subsequently taxed under the CGT regime.

👆 TAX FACT

For tax purposes the ATO requires you to keep a record of:

- the dates, amounts and number of ESS interests that were acquired, exercised or sold
- the amount of the discount you received on the date of acquisition
- the ESS rules
- details of elections made to include discounts in the year of acquisition for interests acquired before 1 July 2009.

The tax rules for the different types of ESS are:

- Taxed upfront
  - The discount you receive is assessable in the financial year you acquired the ESS interests.
  - You are eligible for a $1000 reduction if your taxable income after adjustments is less than $180 000 and you don't hold or control more than 5 per cent of the company.
  - For CGT purposes, the interest is taken to have been acquired at market value on the day it was originally acquired.

- Tax deferred
  - If you acquire less than $5000 of shares via salary sacrifice, or if there is a real risk of forfeiture, the tax on any discount is deferred until the 'deferred taxing point' for a maximum of 15 years after you acquire the share/right.
  - The amount assessed will be the market value of the ESS interests at the deferred taxing point, reduced by the cost base.
  - If you dispose of an ESS interest within 30 days after a deferred taxing point occurred, the date of that disposal becomes the deferred taxing point (known as the '30-day rule').
  - For CGT purposes the interest is taken to have been reacquired immediately after the deferred taxing point in order to determine any eligibility for the 50 per cent CGT discount.

🖆 TAX FACT

Options issued after 30 June 2015 to employees of start-up companies — defined as those less than 10 years old and with an annual turnover of less than $50 million — will be taxed when they are converted to shares (rather than at the time that the option is originally received). Employees who exercise these options after a minimum of three years will also get a 15 per cent tax deduction (with the Commissioner being allowed to exercise discretion in circumstances outside the employees' control that make the minimum three-year holding period impossible to meet). Where options are converted into shares and the resulting shares are sold within 12 months of exercise, the CGT discount concession will be available.

🖆 TAX FACT

You should receive an ESS statement from your employer if you participated in an ESS in order to finalise your income tax return.

Oliver works for XYZ Ltd and acquires 500 shares in XYZ under a taxed-upfront share scheme on 29 July 2025. The total market value of the shares is $5000. Oliver is required to pay $2800 to purchase the shares — thus acquiring the shares for a discount of $2200.

Oliver's adjusted taxable income (including the $2200 discount) is $71000 so he is eligible for the upfront concession of $1000 in his 2025–26 tax return. For CGT purposes, his cost base is $5000.

⚠ PITFALL

When ESS interests are acquired by your spouse, you still need to include the discount in your own tax return but your spouse would be subject to any CGT in the future.

53 SHARE PORTFOLIOS WITHIN SELF MANAGED SUPERANNUATION FUNDS

Earlier in part V, we looked at the merits of having a share portfolio in a low-income earner's name and the taxes that can be saved as a result. There are similar benefits with having shares held by a self managed superannuation fund (SMSF).

♀ TIP

Capital gains on share disposals are taxed at either 10 per cent or 15 per cent in a super fund, which is substantially lower than the 23.5 per cent or 47 per cent that you potentially could be taxed at if you held shares as an individual.

As super funds only pay a flat 15 per cent tax on their income, shares that pay fully franked dividends are quite attractive as imputation credits have a 30 per cent tax credit attached to them. This means that the imputation credit not only covers the tax on the dividend but can also be offset against other income earned by the fund.

In the accumulation stage, an SMSF pays tax at 15 per cent on its taxable income. Any capital gains on investments held for more than 12 months are taxed at only 10 per cent. This is substantially lower than the marginal tax rates for those taxpayers earning over $45 000. And once a pension is started, provided its balance is under $2 million as at 1 July 2025 (or subsequent date that the transfer balance account is created), a fund pays no tax at all on its income or its capital gains.

💡 TIP

When an SMSF goes into a pension phase, it provides a special opportunity to avoid CGT altogether on a share portfolio as no tax is payable when shares are sold during this stage, provided the fund balance is under $2 million as at 1 July 2025 (or subsequent date that the transfer balance account is created).

An investment strategy where there is a share portfolio generating predominantly franked dividend income is quite tax-friendly in an SMSF. The fund receives excess franking credits on the difference between the 30 per cent company tax attached to the dividends and its 15 per cent tax rate. The dividends are effectively tax-free and these excess credits can be used to reduce tax on other fund income.

SMSF members are allowed to transfer shares into the fund 'in-specie' unlike property. There are contribution limits as to the number of shares that can be transferred at market value each year. Depending on the personal tax situation of the member, the transfer may be tax-deductible at the taxpayer's marginal tax rate but assessable to the fund at 15 per cent (increasing to 30 per cent for individuals with income greater than $250 000).

54 CRYPTOCURRENCY

It's amazing how the financial world evolves. When I wrote the first edition of this book in 2011 I would have been more likely to write about kryptonite and its impact on super rather than cryptocurrency.

Bitcoin. Ethereum. Litecoin. Tether. Dogecoin. Ripple. EOS. The cryptocurrency (or altcoin) list seems to get added to almost by the week. Okay I will admit, I hardly know anything about them. But as they are digital assets which people invest or trade in then we do need to worry about their treatment for taxation purposes.

The ATO's interpretation on the tax treatment of cryptocurrency is slowly evolving as transactions in cryptocurrency become more and more common. Although it does vary from crypto to crypto, the ATO's view is that they are neither 'money' nor 'currency' but rather 'property' and are assets which are taxable under CGT regulations.

Each cryptocurrency has its own unique features which may result in a different tax treatment to other digital assets.

The tax treatment of cryptocurrency will also vary depending if you acquired it for:

- personal use
- investment
- trading
- business income and expenses.

Regardless of your situation ensure that you keep records in relation to your acquiring or disposing of cryptocurrency transactions.

A CGT event occurs when you dispose of your cryptocurrency. If you make a capital gain on the disposal of a cryptocurrency, some or all of the gain may be taxed. Certain capital gains or losses that arise from the disposal of cryptocurrency that is a personal use asset may be disregarded.

Only capital gains you make from personal use assets acquired for more than $10 000 are taxable for CGT purposes. However, all capital losses you make on personal use assets are disregarded.

Cryptocurrency is not a personal use asset if it is acquired, kept or used:

- as an investment
- in a profit-making scheme
- in the course of carrying on a business.

● TAX FACT

If you acquire a cryptocurrency purely to purchase items for personal use or consumption – and it was acquired for under $10 000 – then any capital gain can be disregarded for tax purposes.

● TAX FACT

According to CoinGecko there were 17139 cryptocurrencies across 1296 exchanges with a total market capitalisation of $2.78 trillion as at April 2025. Bitcoin is the dominant cryptocurrency with its market cap accounting for 59.85 per cent of the total market.

Similar to the discussion about share traders and share investors (see p. 138), if the disposal of your cryptocurrency is part of a business you carry on, the profits you make on disposal will be treated as ordinary income and not as a capital gain.

✋ TAX FACT

To be classed as a cryptocurrency trader for tax purposes, you need to demonstrate to the ATO that you:

• carry on your activity for commercial reasons and in a commercially viable way

• undertake activities in a business-like manner. This would typically include preparing a business plan and acquiring capital assets or inventory in line with the business plan

• prepare accounting records and market a business name or product

• intend to make a profit or genuinely believe you will make a profit, even if you are unlikely to do so in the short term.

There's usually repetition and regularity to your business activities, although one-off transactions can amount to a business in some cases.

If you are considered to be a cryptocurrency investor then you are not entitled to the personal use asset exemption and may have to pay tax on any capital gain you make on its disposal. Just like with investments properties or shares, you will be eligible for the 50 per cent CGT discount on any gain (see p. 108) if you hold for the cryptocurrency for more than 12 months. If you make a capital loss then it can be used to reduce capital gains made in the same year or in future years. Net capital losses cannot be offset against other income.

✋ TAX FACT

If you receive additional tokens via airdrops or staking rewards then the ATO may deem these as assessable income at the time derived. The cost base of the new tokens is deemed to be their market value at the time derived. By contrast, chain splits do not constitute a taxable event at the time of receipt.

If you lose your private key or your cryptocurrency is stolen then you may be able to claim the capital loss.

⚠ PITFALL

If you dispose of one cryptocurrency to acquire another cryptocurrency directly, the ATO will deem this to be a capital gains tax event despite not trading via Australian dollars.

✋ TAX FACT

Unlike with share splits where you apportion the cost base between the two stocks, the cost base of a new crypto asset that you receive as a result of a chain split is zero. You will only be potentially eligible for the 50 per cent CGT discount if you hold the new crypto asset for more than 12 months.

⚠ PITFALL

You need to keep the following records in relation to your cryptocurrency transactions:

- the date of each transaction
- the value of the cryptocurrency in Australian dollars at the time of the transaction (which can be taken from a reputable online exchange)
- what the transaction was for and who the other party was (even if it's just their cryptocurrency address).

If you receive cryptocurrency for goods or services you provide as part of your business, you need to include the value of the cryptocurrency in Australian dollars as part of your ordinary income. This is the same process as receiving any other non–cash consideration under a barter transaction.

There may be some CGT and income tax implications if you incorporate decentralised finance (DeFi) in your crypto activities. DeFi is an Ethereum blockchain-based form of finance that is conducted without relying on a financial intermediary. When you lend to a DeFi platform there is a deemed disposal of your coins which triggers a capital gain or loss and a subsequent new cost base on the re-acquisition when the loan is repaid. When interest is paid in the form of newly issued coin tokens, you will need to declare the market value of those tokens as assessable income (which also becomes their cost base for CGT purposes).

I have been regularly acquiring cryptocurrency for over six months with the intention of selling at a favourable exchange rate. Instead of cashing out the gains and paying tax at year end, can I buy some goods and services directly for personal use and avoid tax altogether?

Nice try but unfortunately not. The ATO will view that you purchased the cryptocurrency initially as an investment and any gain realised would be assessable for CGT purposes. The fact that you subsequently used the cryptocurrency for personal use purchases does not make it a personal use asset and exempt for CGT purposes (assuming that it was less than $10 000).

According to a Swyftx Australian Digital Assets Survey, it is estimated that 20 per cent of Australians own cryptocurrency as at August 2024.

The ATO's datamatching program has both personal and transaction details on 1.2 million Australian cryptocurrency users. It compares that data against lodged tax returns and has contacted more than 200 000 taxpayers who have traded in cryptocurrency dating back to the 2014–15 year to remind them of their tax obligations and to review their returns. Any taxpayer who chooses to ignore the ATO's letter (that is, they do not amend their tax return for any capital gain or loss incurred) may receive further scrutiny including an audit of their affairs.

55 NON-FUNGIBLE TOKENS

The latest technology trend being traded are non-fungible tokens (NFT) which are units of data that are stored on a blockchain/digital ledger which can represent unique digital items — such as digital pictures of art, audio and video clips, video games, memes, plus other forms of creative work. Unlike cryptocurrencies, an NFT is a cryptographic asset which is not mutually interchangeable/fungible in the same way that cryptocurrency coins and tokens are.

I will be the first one to admit that when I saw the name of these I thought of mushrooms, so you can imagine my surprise when my Google search for NFTs produced a series of 3D animated images of mushrooms! Like a mushroom, you could be left in the dark if you don't consider the tax implications of holding NFTs.

✋ TAX FACT

The ATO have announced that the tax treatment of NFTs follow the same general principles as cryptocurrencies.

Similar to cryptocurrency, the tax treatment of an NFT depends on your reason for holding and using NFTs as well as how you transact with them, although it is unlikely that they will be considered a personal use asset.

Typically, NFTs will either be treated as part of a business operation with its revenue being treated as trading income or it will be considered a capital asset and potentially subject to capital gains tax on disposal.

♀ TIP

After becoming an overnight sensation when they first came out, NFTs popularity have waned significantly in recent times with sale prices falling across the board, so there may be significant losses being accrued by holders. If you have made other capital gains during the year, then consider disposing these tokens to reduce your potential liability.

Conversely, if you were fortunate to get an NFT at a bargain under your own name, consider holding it for more than 12 months in order to obtain the 50 per cent CGT discount. If you purchased it in a company's name, then the organisation is not able to receive the concession.

👍 TAX FACT

The ATO does not consider NFTs as a form of digital currency. As a result, GST may be applicable on their disposal if you are operating an NFT business.

⚠ PITFALL

Although there is a possibility that you can pay for an NFT with cash, most marketplaces often set prices in cryptocurrency. This adds to the risk in holding them as you may have a raw gain negated purely due to fall in value of the cryptocurrency that you trade in, adding to complexity when calculating gains or losses for tax purposes.

PART VI

YOUR SUPERANNUATION

Superannuation is money set aside throughout your working life to provide for your retirement. Behind the family home, it's the second-largest asset for many Australians, maybe even the largest. But it is ridiculous how little attention is paid to it. You need to take the time to look after one of your biggest assets. It doesn't need much. If you don't have enough money in super to look after yourself when you retire there are government pensions to support you.

🔖 TAX FACT

As at 31 December 2024, the total assets within Australian superannuation were $4.167 trillion (Australian Prudential Regulation Authority 2025b), which was greater than the market capitalisation of the Australian equities market of $3.007 trillion (Australian Securities Exchange 2025), the combined deposits on the books of all Australian banks of $3.102 trillion (Australian Prudential Regulation Authority 2025a) and the Gross Domestic Product of Australia of $2.617 trillion (Australian Bureau of Statistics 2025).

Figure 6.1 (overleaf) reports the movement in total assets held by the various segments of the Australian superannuation industry since 1996. Total assets in the industry have grown from $245.5 billion to $4166.9 billion as at 31 December 2024, the number of funds rising almost sixfold from 105 377 in 1996 to 638 411 funds and the number of member accounts doubling during the period to approximately 32 million (Australian Prudential Regulation Authority 2025b). The economic significance of the superannuation industry in Australia, measured by assets in the industry as a proportion of GDP, has jumped from 37.9 per cent in 1996 to 159.22 per cent in December 2024 (Australian Bureau of Statistics 2025). A notable feature of figure 6.1 is the rapid growth of the SMSF sector over the past decade, which now comprises the second largest segment of the superannuation industry (by assets) behind industry funds. Funds under management in the SMSF sector have risen from $60.9 billion (330000 members in 166475 funds) in 1999/2000 to $980.9 billion (1184287 members in 638411 funds) in December 2024 (Australian Taxation Office 2025). SMSFs now account for 24.4 per cent of assets in the Australian pension industry and 99.8 per cent of funds, compared with 50.60 per cent and 0.006 per cent for not-for-profit (corporate plus public sector plus industry) funds and 19.35 per cent and 0.009 per cent for retail funds.

FIGURE 6.1: superannuation industry in Australia 1996–2024 by total assets ($ billion)

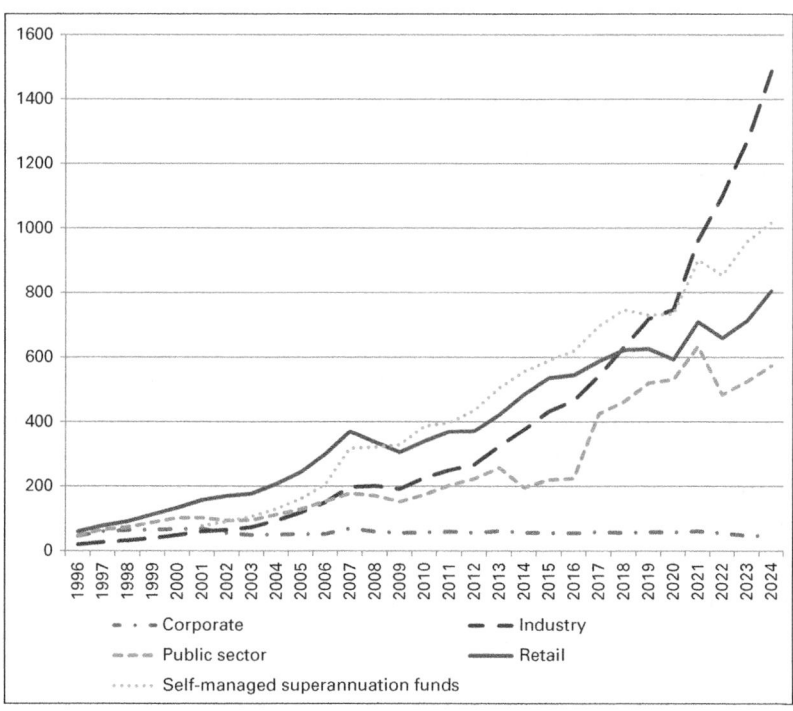

Sources: Arnold et al. (2015), Bird et al. (2018), Raftery (2014), Thorp et al. (2020), Australian Prudential Regulatory Authority (2025b)

It is never too late to start putting money into super, but the earlier you can start the better because small amounts added when you are young can make a big difference to the size of your savings in retirement.

Super funds can invest in shares, property, term deposits and managed funds and they enjoy very generous tax concessions, with complying super funds receiving more favourable tax treatment than companies and individuals earning over $18 200.

👆 TAX FACT

The tax rate for a complying superannuation fund on its net income and contributions is 15 per cent. Contributions are taxed at 30 per cent if they are for individuals with income greater than $250 000. Capital gains tax is reduced to 10 per cent when assets are held for at least one year.

Part VI will focus on different ways to give your super a boost and how to access it in the most tax–effective way.

⚠ PITFALL

Before you roll over monies into a new super fund, check to see if you have an insurance policy attached to your existing fund. People with longstanding insurance cover will need to renew it if they move into an SMSF, and may fail new conditions such as declaring pre-existing conditions. Ask your old fund if there is a 'continuation option' that will allow you to buy a private policy without having to provide medical evidence.

💡 TIP

If you start a new job, chances are that you are earning more than your previous role. How about using some of that money to make extra contributions to superannuation via salary sacrifice? The sooner you start saving, the bigger your retirement kitty will be.

56 CONTRIBUTION LIMITS

The quickest way to grow your super fund balance is to make significant contributions into the fund over time and then enjoy the benefits of watching money make money.

💡 TIP

If you earn less than $250000 you can contribute up to $30000 per year into super and only pay 15 per cent tax. While you don't have access today, it is your money and you can build up your net wealth quicker instead of paying up to 47 per cent in tax.

There are two kinds of contribution that can be made to a super fund:

• concessional contributions (before tax)
• non-concessional contributions (after tax).

Concessional contributions, taxed at 15 per cent (or 30 per cent if the individual earns more than $250000), are known as before-tax contributions because the contributor, usually an employer, can claim an income tax deduction for them. The cap for concessional contributions is $30000 per year. They include all compulsory super guarantee contributions, salary-sacrifice contributions, and any personal contributions that you intend to claim as a tax deduction.

Non-concessional contributions are not taxed by the ATO and they include personal contributions you make after tax.

The ATO caps the non-concessional contributions you can make each year before you pay extra tax to four times the concessional contributions cap (that is, $120 000). Additionally, the non-concessional cap is restricted to people with superannuation balances less than $2 million at the end of the previous financial year. The untaxed plan cap of benefits that have not been subject to contributions tax within a super fund is $1 865 000.

If you are under 75 years old for at least one day of the financial year and your superannuation balance is no more than $1.76 million, you can bring forward two years' worth of contributions, giving you a maximum non-concessional contributions cap of $360000 in the current year (with nothing in the following two years if the whole amount is contributed in the first year of the period), rather than a $120000 cap in each of the three years. Table 6.1 shows that the maximum non-concessional cap that you can bring forward reduces when superannuation balances are over $1.76 million. The period begins in the first year that you contribute more than the non-concessional contribution cap.

TABLE 6.1: non-concessional contribution limits under bring forward period rule (2025–26)

Total superannuation balance prior year	Maximum non-concessional contribution cap	Bring-forward period
< $1760000	$360000	3 years
$1760000–$1879999	$240000	2 years
$1880000–$1999999	$120000	nil
> $2000000	nil	nil

Source: © Australian Taxation Office for the Commonwealth of Australia.

Since 1 January 2023, if you are aged 55 and over and you sell your family home of at least ten years, you can make a 'downsizer' non-concessional contribution of up to $300000 regardless of how much super you have.

👍 **TAX FACT**

The date that your super fund receives your contributions can also be important as contributions are counted towards the caps in the year in which they are received and credited by your super fund. A cheque sent at the end of June but not received by the super fund until July will count towards the next financial year's cap.

Excess concessional contributions are included in an individual's taxable income and taxed at their marginal tax rate (plus an interest charge) regardless of their income or the cause of the breach. The individual can choose to pay the tax bill from their own sources, or use their after-tax excess concessional contribution from super. Since 1 July 2021, individuals are no longer liable to pay an excess concessional contribution charge should they exceed their cap.

57 TRANSFER BALANCE CAP

Anyone who knows me will tell you that I have been harping on for years about how superannuation is one of the very best places to save money on your tax legally especially with no tax to pay on your savings in retirement mode. Unfortunately, a few took full advantage of the generous loophole by placing millions upon millions into super to avoid paying any tax at all. So it came as no surprise that the regulators tried to limit this loophole by placing a cap from 1 July 2017 on how much super you can have in retirement without paying tax.

The transfer balance cap is a limit – currently $2 million – on how much superannuation can be transferred from your accumulation super account to a tax-free 'retirement phase' account. It will be indexed to CPI, rounded down to the nearest $100 000. All your account balances are included when working out this amount. It does not matter how many accounts you hold these balances in.

If you exceed your transfer balance cap, you may have to convert a portion of your retirement phase income stream into a lump sum accumulation account and pay tax on the notional earnings related to that excess. It still remains an attractive concession with the tax rate only being 15 per cent on the excess with earnings on the first $2 million (or $4 million for couples) being tax-free.

The imposition of the $2 million transfer balance cap means that some assets which exceed the cap will need to be moved from pension mode back into accumulation mode. If an SMSF uses the segregation of assets method, then moving assets back into accumulation mode could provide the opportunity for the SMSF to keep assets that might incur a capital gains tax liability in pension mode whilst transferring assets which are unlikely to incur a capital gains tax liability – or will produce lower income (for example cash and fixed interest investments) – back into accumulation mode.

With a $2 million transfer balance cap on superannuation, there is an opportunity to split superannuation contributions between spouses such that each spouse maximises their respective $2 million thresholds (that is, $4 million in total) before they retire.

If you have an excess transfer balance it is important to transfer the money from retirement phase as soon as possible to limit the amount of excess transfer balance tax payable. The tax payable is determined by calculating daily notional earnings based on the General Interest Charge rate (currently 11.17 per cent). The tax rate is 15 per cent for the first time you have an excess transfer balance which doubles to 30 per cent if you go over the transfer balance cap again.

Limited recourse borrowing arrangements are included in a member's total superannuation and $2 million transfer balance cap calculations.

The government has proposed that from 1 July 2025 an additional Div 296 tax of 15 per cent will apply to an adjusted earnings figure for superannuation balances for individuals exceeding $3 million. It is proposed that the adjusted earnings will correspond to the proportion of an individual's total superannuation balance above $3 million. If the adjusted earnings results in a loss then it is proposed that the member will be entitled to carry forward the adjusted loss to offset tax in future years. If this proposal gets enacted then it is an even greater incentive to split superannuation between spouses and take advantage of a combined $6 million balance.

58 DOWNSIZER CONTRIBUTION

From reducing the concessional and non-concessional caps through to introducing the transfer balance cap, the Government has tightened the number of ways that people can pump money into super over the last ten years. However, this trend was reversed when the 2017–18 federal budget announced the opportunity for senior Australians to boost their super balance by being able to contribute some or all of the proceeds from the sale of their own house into superannuation without impacting on pre-existing concessional or non-concessional caps. Initially the concession was only available to those aged 65 and over but those aged 55 and over can now access it.

👆 **TAX FACT**

Since 1 January 2023, individuals aged 55 and over who meet the eligibility requirements will be able to make a non-concessional contribution of up to $300 000 from the sale proceeds of a principal residence that has been held for at least 10 years. These contributions will be in addition to existing caps and are exempt from the age and work tests as well as the $2 million transfer balance cap.

Although this contribution is known as a 'downsizer' contribution it is not a requirement to actually 'downsize' to a smaller place, nor is there a need to actually buy a new home in the first instance.

Your downsizer contribution is not a non-concessional contribution and will not count towards your contributions caps. The downsizer contribution can still be made even if you have a total super balance greater than $2 million.

👍 TAX FACT

Since 1 January 2023 the minimum age to be able to make a downsizer contribution was lowered to 55 years.

👍 TAX FACT

You will be eligible to make a downsizer contribution to super if all of the following conditions apply:

- you are 55 years old or older at the time you make a downsizer contribution (there is no maximum age limit nor any work test requirement)
- the amount you are contributing is from the proceeds of selling your home where the contract of sale exchanged on or after 1 July 2018
- your home was owned by you or your spouse for 10 years or more prior to the sale (calculated from the dates of settlement of the original purchase and eventual sale)
- your home is in Australia
- your home is not a caravan, houseboat or other mobile home
- the net proceeds from the sale of the home are either exempt or partially exempt from CGT under the main residence exemption
- the contribution is a maximum of $300 000 and must be no more than the net proceeds from the sale of your home
- you complete a downsizer contribution into super form by the time the contribution is made
- the contribution is made within 90 days from the date of settlement
- you have not previously made a downsizer contribution to super from the sale of another home (that is, there is a limit of one downsizer into super event in your lifetime).

Your spouse can also contribute up to $300 000 as a downsizer contribution even if your home that was sold was only owned by you and your spouse that did not have an ownership interest and provided they meet all of the other requirements listed above.

It is important to note that the downsizer contribution will count towards your transfer balance cap but your total super balance will only be recalculated on 30 June at the end of the financial year. Downsizer contributions will be taken into account for determining eligibility for the age pension so it would be wise to consult a financial adviser to be fully aware of any impact to the age pension assets test prior to selling and making such a contribution.

Although a downsizer contribution needs to be made within 90 days of receiving the proceeds of sale, the ATO will allow you to apply for a longer period if required because of circumstances outside your control. The request should be made within the initial 90-day timeframe and it will usually be granted due to ill health, a death in the family, or moving house.

It is possible to make multiple downsizer contributions but they must all come from the proceeds of a single sale and the total of all your contributions must not exceed $300 000 or the total proceeds of the sale less any other downsizer contributions that have been made by your spouse.

A downsizer contribution into super form needs to be submitted to your superannuation fund by the time you make your contribution. False and misleading penalties may be applied if the ATO subsequently determines that your downsizer contribution was not eligible. In this situation the ATO will notify your superannuation fund and the fund will need to assess whether your contribution could have been made as a personal contribution. If it could be accepted as a personal contribution, it will count towards the relevant contributions cap. If it cannot be accepted, then your super fund will need to return your contribution.

? FAQ

If I sell my home of 30 years four months before my 55th birthday, can I request an extension from the ATO to make my downsizer contribution until after I turn 55?

You can by all means ask the ATO but the reality is that the ATO would deny such a request merely to allow you to meet the age requirement. I would suggest deferring the settlement to such time that it's within 90 days of your 55th birthday.

59 COMPULSORY EMPLOYER CONTRIBUTIONS

When you are employed, your employer must pay super (known as superannuation guarantee (SG) contributions) on your behalf into a complying super fund. The introduction of the compulsory SG in 1992 has seen a huge boost in superannuation balances for Australians over the past two decades.

SG contributions are paid every quarter by your employer at a minimum of 12 per cent of your ordinary time earnings in 2025–26, up to the maximum contribution base. The payments count towards your concessional contributions cap. You may be able to choose the fund that this super is paid into, provided it is a complying super fund.

● TAX FACT

The government has strengthened the tax laws to counter fraudulent phoenix activity (where companies intentionally accumulate debts to improve cash flow or wealth and then liquidate to avoid paying the debt). The law changes are designed to protect workers' entitlements and strengthen directors' obligations by:

- extending the director penalty regime and the estimates regime to include the unpaid superannuation guarantee charge
- ensuring that directors cannot discharge their director penalties by placing their company into administration or liquidation when any pay as you go (PAYG) withholding or superannuation guarantee charge remains unpaid and unreported three months after the date that it is due for payment
- making directors and their associates liable to PAYG withholding non-compliance tax.

Contractors who are paid wholly or principally for their labour are considered employees for SG purposes and must have 12 per cent SG contributions paid on their behalf under the same scenario as employees.

Ordinary time earnings are used to work out any SG contributions payable for employees. They are usually what you earn during ordinary hours of work and include allowances, bonuses, commissions and any over-award payments. Ordinary time earnings exclude annual leave loadings, expense reimbursements and any overtime payments.

👆 TAX FACT

Superannuation contributions made from personal injury payments are excluded from counting towards your non-concessional contributions cap for a financial year.

👆 TAX FACT

Employers must include the date that they intend to pay accrued superannuation on payslips provided to employees. Employers must also advise of the date that they last paid contributions on behalf of employees.

60 SALARY SACRIFICE

Perhaps the most tax-effective way to contribute money into super is via salary-sacrifice contributions, where you enter into an agreement with your employer to have some of your salary paid into your super fund instead of being paid to you. This has significant tax advantages if you earn over $18 200 (where the marginal tax rate jumps from zero to 21 per cent) as the contribution into super is only taxed at 15 per cent. Salary-sacrifice contributions count towards the concessional contributions cap.

♀ TIP

Salary sacrificing into superannuation is one of the best legitimate ways of minimising your income tax bill.

The benefits of salary sacrificing include:

* super contributions are deductible for your employer

- your assessable income is reduced and potentially subject to a lower marginal rate
- money put into super is only taxed at 15 per cent instead of your marginal tax rate (potentially 47 per cent).

✎ EXAMPLE

In the 2025–26 year, Joan and Cleo both work at XYZ Ltd, earning $69 000 a year with $7935 in compulsory SG contributions. Cleo entered into a salary-sacrifice arrangement with her employer to sacrifice $22 065 of her earnings into her super fund to top up her concessional contributions to $30 000. Joan didn't salary sacrifice any of her salary.

Table 6.2 shows the difference between Joan's and Cleo's assessable incomes and rates of tax at the end of the income year.

TABLE 6.2: example of salary-sacrifice benefits

	Joan	Cleo
Gross salary	$69 000	$69 000
Less super salary sacrifice	—	$22 065
Assessable income	$69 000	$46 935
Deductions	$1000	$1000
Taxable income	$68 000	$45 935
Income tax	$11 188	$4569
Medicare levy (2%)	$1360	$919
Tax on super contribution (15%)	—	$3310
Less: low-income tax offset	—	$311
Total tax paid	**$12 548**	**$8486**

Source: © Australian Taxation Office for the Commonwealth of Australia.

♀ TIP

Effective from 2018–19, you can carry forward any unused amounts from your annual concessional contribution limit of $30 000 (previously $27 500) to future years. This carry forward concessional contribution rule is only available for a maximum of five years for individuals with superannuation balances under $500 000 at the start of each financial year.

✎ EXAMPLE

Rashid's employer paid $9000 of SG contributions into his super-annuation account during the 2025–26 financial year. He made no other contributions that year and had a total of $34 000 in super. For the 2026–27 financial year Rashid's concessional contribution limit increases to $51 000 — being the standard $30 000 limit plus $21 000 unused limit carried forward from the prior year. If he elects to put nothing extra that year – other than his employer's $9000 of SG contributions again – then as table 6.3 shows, his adjusted concessional contribution limit in the 2027–28 year will be $72 000. If he has another $9000 of SG contributions in 2027–28 then he can salary sacrifice a further $63 000 that year.

TABLE 6.3: example of carry forward concessional contributions

	2025–26	2026–27	2027–28
Employer contributions	$9000	$9000	$9000
Super salary sacrifice	—	—	$63 000
Total concessional contributions	$9000	$9000	$72 000
Unused concessional limit for year	$21 000	$21 000	—
Carried forward concessional limit	$21 000	$42 000	—

⚠ PITFALL

If you earn under $22 575 you are better off taking your money rather than salary sacrificing extra into super as you are effectively paying no tax at this level (see p. 15). Don't pay 15 per cent contributions tax when you can pay nil.

On the downside, salary sacrificing into super can have some negatives:

- Any super guarantee payments are based on your reduced salary (unless you negotiate otherwise).
- The salary-sacrificed amount counts towards your employer's super guarantee obligations.

- The concessional tax rate of 15 per cent is capped at $30 000 into super each year. The rate increases to 30 per cent for individuals with income greater than $250 000.
- Any salary-sacrificed amounts will be reportable employer superannuation contributions that are included on your payment summary and will affect the income tests for the Medicare levy surcharge and some tax offsets and government benefits.
- Money can be tied up in super and you have to wait until retirement to access it.
- Payment of the sacrificed amounts above the compulsory SG is not required by regulation to be made quarterly, as is the SG.
- Some employers neglect to pay employees' super, particularly if they are close to bankruptcy and are having cash-flow difficulties.

> **⚠ PITFALL**
>
> Salary sacrifice is a relatively straightforward strategy, but it's crucial that you crunch the numbers correctly because any contributions made that exceed the respective cap will be taxed at 47 per cent rather than the 15 per cent (or 30 per cent) concessional tax rate.

61 DIVISION 293 TAX

Over the years there has been a great incentive for those taxpayers on the top marginal tax rate of 47 per cent to whack in as much money as possible into super and be taxed at the more generous concessional tax rate of 15 per cent and essentially locking in a 32 per cent tax saving on any contributions. This benefit was recently reduced but not totally diminished with the introduction of Division 293 into the Tax Act.

Division 293 tax is an additional tax on super contributions which reduces the tax concession for individuals whose combined adjusted taxable income and contributions are greater than the Division 293 threshold of $250000. Division 293 tax is charged at an additional 15 per cent (effectively 30 per cent in total) of an individual's taxable contributions during the financial year that they exceeded the $250000 threshold. There is no Division 293 tax to pay if you did not have any taxable contributions in the year.

⚠ PITFALL

Even though your income may not normally be in excess of $250000, certain events can increase it to beyond this level for a particular year including eligible termination payments and capital gains. In these situations you will be liable for the extra 15 per cent Division 293 tax on your contributions into super for that year.

🕯 TAX FACT

Division 293 tax is only levied on your concessional contributions for the year. There is no tax on non-concessional contributions and any earnings are subject to the standard 15 per cent concessional tax rate.

If you are over the income threshold, the ATO will issue a Division 293 notice generally several months after the end of the financial year once they match your tax return with information sent to them by your super fund on contributions made. You can elect to have monies released from your super fund to pay the amount outstanding rather than using your own funds.

If the extra tax payable relates to a defined benefit interest then the debt is deferred until a super benefit is paid with interest accruing based on the average 10-year Treasury bond rate (currently 4.31 per cent).

♀ TIP

If you expect to have a Division 293 tax payable and you operate a self-managed superannuation fund, consider an investment strategy which generates fully franked dividends with imputation credits at 30 per cent to partially or wholly negate the impact of the additional tax.

If you run your own business, consider varying the amount of income (either via wages or dividends) that you withdraw from the company each year to minimise the impact of the Division 293 tax. It is much better to have an adjusted taxable income just below the $250 000 for nine out of ten years with one year totally blowing the threshold level out of the water (for example, 9 lots of $200 000 then $1.2 million) rather than having your income sitting just above the $250 000 threshold for each of the ten years (for example, $300 000 per annum).

62 SUPER CO-CONTRIBUTION

The term 'super co-contribution' should really be labelled as 'free money'! But it is surprising how few people actually take advantage of this great benefit.

Super co-contribution has been a government initiative since 2005 to help grow the superannuation balances for low and middle income earners. If you earn less than $62 488, you can take advantage of the super co-contribution payment by making a maximum personal super contribution of $1000 into your super fund. The government will then match it by 50 per cent up to a further $500.

⚠ PITFALL

The super co-contribution is only available to those with a total superannuation balance of less than the transfer balance cap of $2 000 000 at the end of the previous financial year. It is also unavailable if you have already reached your non-concessional contributions cap for the year.

If you qualify for the co-contribution, you do not need to do anything other than make the actual personal super contributions to your super fund and lodge your income tax return. There is no separate form or application to complete. The personal super contribution must be paid into a complying super fund and must not have been claimed as an income tax deduction. You can contact your super fund to find out how to make such a contribution.

> **♀ TIP**
>
> At the start of each tax year, organise with your payroll department to have $20 taken out of your pay each week as a post-tax contribution into superannuation. You will find that this is a lot easier than trying to find $1000 in the last week in June.

The ATO outlines the two income tests you must satisfy to be eligible for the super co-contribution:

- the income threshold test
- the 10 per cent eligible income test.

The income threshold test

According to the ATO, if your total income (assessable income plus reportable fringe benefits total plus reportable employer super contributions less allowable deductions) is under the lower income threshold of $47 488 and you contribute $1000 post-tax into your super fund, the government will match it with a further $500. The super co-contribution gradually phases out to nil (by 3.333 cents per dollar) at the higher income threshold of $62 488.

> **✎ EXAMPLE**
>
> Luke is an employee whose assessable income, reportable fringe benefits and reportable super contributions total $49 000. During the 2025–26 year he contributes $3000 as a personal super contribution to his super fund.
>
> Luke will receive $450 from the government as a co-contribution calculated as follows:
>
> $$\$500 - [(\$49\,000 - \$47\,488) \times \$0.03333]$$

The 10 per cent eligible income test

The ATO outlines that at least 10 per cent of your total income (assessable income plus reportable fringe benefits total plus reportable employer super contributions) must come from employment-related activities or carrying on a business, otherwise you will not be eligible for the co-contribution.

⚠ PITFALL

You are not entitled to a super co-contribution for any personal contributions that you have chosen to claim and that have been allowed as a tax deduction.

☝ TAX FACT

You need to provide your TFN to your super fund before it can accept any personal super contributions, including the superannuation co-contribution. There is no tax on these contributions.

If you don't see any super co-contribution payment on your annual super fund statement (or it is different from what you have calculated), contact the ATO.

? FAQ

My teenage daughter works part-time after school. Can she put money into super and get the co-contribution from the government or does she need to wait until she is over 18?

There are three key conditions in order to be eligible for the co-contribution. First, you must make a post-tax (non-concessional) contribution into your super fund. Second, you must be under 71 years of age. Finally, you must pass the two income tests — the 10 per cent eligible income and threshold (under $62 488) tests. As your daughter should satisfy all of these conditions I would recommend that she puts up to $1000 into her super fund so that the government matches it with an extra $500.

63 TRANSFERRING FOREIGN SUPER

Many Australians have worked overseas and accrued retirement benefits in foreign super funds. Depending on the rules of your foreign super fund you may be able to transfer an amount from a foreign super fund to either a complying Australian super fund or yourself.

⚠ PITFALL

The transferred amounts will count towards your contributions caps, outlined earlier, and you may have to pay excess contributions tax if they exceed these caps. You or your fund may have to pay income tax on some or the entire amount. There may also be some tax obligations in the foreign country.

Prior to your Australian super fund accepting any transfer of foreign super monies, the following conditions must be met:

- *Age.* Contributions, other than SG contributions where there is no age limit, can be accepted if you are under 75.
- *TFN.* You have provided your TFN to your super fund.
- *Contribution limit.* The transfer doesn't exceed your fund-capped contribution limit. If you are under 75 you could potentially bring-forward three years of the cap, dependent on your superannuation balance.

✎ EXAMPLE

Pierre is 71 and in May 2025 he transfers his super interest of $468000 from France to Australia. Over his lifetime he has made non-concessional contributions of $320000 to Australian funds, but none in the last five years. As he is under 75 he cannot contribute more than the first $360000 (being the $120000 annual non-concessional limit brought forward for three years), he must return the excess $108000 to his French super fund. He would need to wait til after 1 July 2028 before he could transfer the balance.

You also need to pay income tax on the 'applicable fund earnings' component of a foreign fund transfer. These are the earnings on your foreign super balance that have accrued only since you became an Australian resident. None of your foreign super is treated as applicable fund earnings if you transfer it to Australia within six months of becoming an Australian resident.

> **♀TIP**
>
> If you elect to include some of your applicable fund earnings in your super fund's assessable income, rather than your own, your fund will pay the tax on the amount at 15 per cent, which could be less than the marginal rate of tax that you have to pay.

✏ EXAMPLE

Ryan emigrated to Australia in September 2010 when his foreign super balance was the equivalent of A$250 000. In May 2026, he transferred the balance to his Australian super fund when it was valued at A$350 000.

If Ryan makes no election, he must declare the $100 000 of 'applicable fund earnings' in his personal assessable income for the year which is taxed at his marginal tax rates. If he elects to include the applicable fund earnings into his super fund's assessable income, it is taxed at 15 per cent within the fund.

64 SELF MANAGED SUPERANNUATION FUNDS

As the name implies, a self managed super fund (SMSF) is a type of super fund that the members manage for their own benefit. SMSFs are growing in popularity as members' balances rise and they become more knowledgeable about managing their retirement savings. Over 33 000 new SMSFs were established in 2023–24 alone. The attractiveness of the concessional tax rules for super funds means that similar growth is expected to continue for some time yet.

If you have the time as well as the expertise, including advisers you can call on, to devote to managing your investments, setting up an SMSF may be an option for you to look at for your retirement future.

Benefits of having an SMSF include:

- freedom to decide how and where to invest your superannuation funds
- tax benefits:
  - the maximum tax payable on contributions is 30 per cent and only 15 per cent for earnings in a complying SMSF. Capital gains tax on assets held more than 12 months is just 10 per cent.
  - earnings (including any capital gains) in the pension phase are not taxable (subject to the fund balance being under $2 million as at 1 July 2025 or subsequent date that the transfer balance account is created)

- economies of scale—when family members (up to four) combine their superannuation funds the whole can become greater than the sum of its parts
- ability to invest in direct share portfolios—resulting imputation credits on dividends can help reduce the overall tax to be paid by the fund
- ability to invest in business real property
- deductible life insurance premiums
- rollover benefits—on retirement, assets can be rolled over into the pension phase and any capital gains subsequently realised will have no tax payable, provided that the fund balance is under $2 million on 1 July 2025 (or subsequent date that the transfer balance account is created). Amounts above this threshold will remain in accumulation phase and be subject to the normal 15 per cent tax on earnings in a complying SMSF.

While SMSFs can be great, they are not ideal for everyone. Before you establish one you should think carefully about some of the following issues:

- *Administrative obligations.* These may be onerous and include:
  - arranging an annual audit of your fund
  - keeping appropriate records
  - reporting to the ATO on the fund's operation.
- *Annual charges.* Fees for administration, accounting, tax and audit can be expensive and range between $2000 and $6000 for an average-sized fund.
- *Compliance.* You need to be aware of the requirements of being an SMSF trustee as you are responsible for ensuring the fund complies with its trust deed and superannuation laws.
- *Management.* You need to manage the fund's investments in the best interests of fund members including ensuring they are for the sole purpose of providing retirement benefits and keeping them separate from the personal and business affairs of fund members.

65 BUYING PROPERTY WITHIN SMSFs

A lot of people say that they don't believe in super and prefer to own bricks and mortar as a means of funding their retirement. But a growing number of people realise they can buy property through the use of their SMSF monies.

'Property is my super' is what they say. But why not property *within* your super?

Property is becoming a very popular asset class in super funds. This is primarily due to favourable tax rates but also because, as super fund balances grow over time, the ability to acquire a property within an SMSF becomes more achievable. Superannuation is also generally protected from 'creditors and predators' and thus makes a secure vehicle for asset protection purposes.

👆 **TAX FACT**

According to the ATO, real property within SMSFs grew from $15.2 billion in 2003–04 to $168 billion in December 2024.

As identified earlier, if you own property in an SMSF, any rental income or gains generated in the SMSF will be concessionally taxed, but once you convert the SMSF into a pension these incomes and gains will become tax-free in the fund, provided the fund balance is under $2 million as at 1 July 2025 (or subsequent date that the transfer balance account is created). Any tax can be reduced depending on the SMSF's investment strategy, such as excess franking credits.

Any SMSF members who receive pension income are concessionally taxed until they reach age 60, at which time this income becomes tax-free to them. With potentially no tax to pay in retirement, there is a sense of utopia while also being able to live in one of the best countries in the world.

An SMSF can purchase any type of property from unrelated parties but can only purchase commercial property, which must be wholly and exclusively used in one or more businesses, from related entities and individuals. It is important that your SMSF has a written investment strategy that allows for the holding of property.

Some issues to consider before owning real property in an SMSF are as follows.

- *Home ownership.* You cannot live in the property owned by your SMSF for private purposes.
- *Related business leases.* Commercial properties can be leased to a related business entity but only if there is a written lease in place.
- *Costs.* Establishment and ongoing annual costs of administration of an SMSF will rise with having a property.
- *Funds.* Your fund must have enough money to effect the purchase of property.
- *Borrowing.* You may consider whether your SMSF should borrow part of the cost to acquire the property.
- *Diversification.* You may consider whether your super fund has an adequate diversification of assets.
- *Liquidation.* You may consider the liquidation of assets required should a member retire or die.

66 GEARING THROUGH A SUPER FUND

They say that money makes money and borrowing is one of the easiest ways of building wealth, particularly within the concessionally taxed environment of superannuation.

> **👆 TAX FACT**
>
> Legislative changes introduced in September 2007 allow SMSFs to borrow via instalment warrants.

A gearing strategy within a super fund is not suitable for everyone as there are risks involved. With an instalment warrant, an SMSF can pay a part of an asset upfront and borrow the rest. While the debt is owing, the asset is held in trust but the SMSF maintains the beneficial interest in it. The SMSF will have the right, but not the obligation, to acquire the legal ownership of the asset through the payment of instalments.

> **💡 TIP**
>
> While there has been anecdotal evidence suggesting that SMSFs borrow significant amounts of money, as at December 2024 there was only $72.0 billion borrowed by SMSFs via limited recourse borrowing arrangements. Hardly a huge amount compared to the amount of property that SMSFs invest in ($168 billion).

If an SMSF acquires a portfolio of shares via an instalment warrant, the SMSF receives dividends that are generally used to pay down the loan. The SMSF may also use instalment warrants to purchase properties.

> **✏ EXAMPLE**
>
> Bob has $400000 of cash sitting in his super fund. His super fund borrows a further $200000, via an instalment warrant, in order to acquire a $600000 property. Rental income, together with further super contributions by Bob, will go towards paying off the borrowing. Interest charged is a tax deduction for the fund.

SMSFs can borrow money only if the purchase is structured correctly, but as banks become a lot more accustomed to lending to SMSFs, this type of borrowing is not as complicated as a few years ago. However it should be noted that in the past year, a number of the major banks in Australia no longer offer finance for new purchases in SMSFs.

There are special rules that govern borrowings within SMSFs, including the following:

- Any borrowing by an SMSF must only be for the acquisition of an asset.
- The lender is limited in recourse to the asset itself and not any other asset of the fund.
- Legal title to the asset must be owned by a custodian trustee explicitly for the benefit of the SMSF.
- Any improvements required for an investment property following its acquisition must be paid using the available resources of the SMSF and not borrowed funds.

♀ TIP

While super funds can gear up to 75 per cent (depending on the borrower's restrictions), you should consider falling asset values and restrict borrowing limits to no more than 50 per cent.

? FAQ

Can my super fund purchase an apartment 'off the plan'?

It is possible but you will need to be careful because there can be some issues along the way. The deposit, stamp duty and any other costs to secure the purchase upfront must be paid using existing cash funds in super. Only when the unit is completed and strata titled can finance be used to complete the purchase. By this stage the value of the property may have fallen dramatically which could have drastic effects on your ability to use borrowed funds to partly finance the purchase. Seeking professional advice is recommended.

67 ACCESSING YOUR SUPER

Provided your super fund's deed allows it, you can access your super:

- when you retire after reaching your preservation age
- when you turn 65
- when you cease an employment arrangement after reaching age 60
- under the transition to retirement rules, while continuing to work.

Your preservation age, different from your pension age, is the age you must reach before you can access your super and depends on when you were born. The preservation age is currently 60.

Whether or not the ATO taxes your withdrawal of super funds will depend on your age and whether your super fund is a taxed or untaxed fund.

Most people have their super monies in a taxed super fund, where tax has already been paid on contributions going in and on earnings derived. If you are 60 years or older, any funds that you withdraw from your super fund will be tax-free if the fund is a taxed source. If you're under 60 the taxable component is treated as assessable income.

Regardless of your age, any income from an untaxed fund needs to be shown as assessable income in your tax return and is taxed at your marginal rate.

While the ability to withdraw up to $20 000 tax-free was a real cashflow lifesaver for a lot of people during the COVID-19 pandemic in 2020, I strongly suggest that you try to return those funds back into super as soon as possible. Superannuation is designed for your retirement savings so any withdrawals made now has a huge impact on your long-term nest egg especially as markets invariably recover. The stockmarkets fell substantially during the COVID-19 pandemic and as a result your super fund balance probably suffered greatly too. Any withdrawal in the low point of the market would have resulted in a crystallisation of those falls as real losses, making it even harder to recoup in the future.

⚠ **PITFALL**

If your super balance falls below $6000, you may no longer have the life insurance coverage that you once had.

💡 **TIP**

It is best to wait until you turn 60 to access your super as there is no tax payable on lump sum withdrawals provided that you satisfy a condition of release.

If you haven't reached preservation age, accessing your super before you retire is only allowed in very limited circumstances, such as you:

- are suffering from severe financial hardship
- are eligible on compassionate grounds
- have a terminal medical condition (certified that you are likely to die within two years)
- have a permanent or temporary incapacity.

You will also need to ask your super fund if you are able to withdraw super prior to reaching preservation age as the fund may have special restrictions attached as well.

68 TRANSITION TO RETIREMENT

Some people simply love their job and don't have any intention to retire. Others would love to reduce the number of hours they work but need the cash to survive. Most people think that you have to retire or resign from your job to trigger a release of your super but under the transition to retirement (TtR) rules, you can withdraw some of your super as regular payments to supplement your income.

> **👆 TAX FACT**
>
> If you were over 60 on 1 July 2024 you can commence a transition to retirement (TtR) pension and access up to 10 per cent of your super each year tax-free to supplement your income. For those that are under 65 and not retired, the earnings on the amount supporting the income stream will be taxed at 15 per cent.

Once you reach your preservation age, you can access your super before you retire but only in the form of a non–commutable income stream and not as a lump sum. So once you turn 60, you can reduce your working hours without leaving your job or reducing your income. If you want, you can also top up your income with a regular income stream from your superannuation savings.

The only specific limit on the amount of super benefits that may be withdrawn each year under the TtR rules is that at least 4 per cent but no more than 10 per cent of the member's account balance at the start of the income year.

TtR income streams are taxed just like all other income streams. If you have reached your preservation age, but are under 65, the taxable part of your income stream will be taxed at your marginal tax rate less a 15 per cent tax offset and earnings within the fund will be taxed concessionally at 15 per cent. Once you turn 65 and have not retired, any income from a taxed super fund will be tax-free.

TtR arrangements can be complex to establish and manage, and it is recommended that you see an expert to help you decide if this is right for you.

69 ACCOUNT-BASED PENSIONS

Some people don't trust themselves with a lump sum and prefer to be disciplined by receiving regular payments. There is no requirement to withdraw all of your super just because you turn a certain age. Instead you may elect to convert up to $2 million of your superannuation balances from the accumulation phase into the pension phase (via a transfer balance account) and start an income stream, such as an account-based pension (previously known as an allocated pension).

Income streams receive favourable tax treatment, another reason why people elect to start an account-based pension. Individuals who cash out their super may have to pay income tax on any earnings but these earnings would be tax-free in a pension environment.

The ATO has outlined that if you reach your preservation age, but are under age 60, the taxable component of your income stream will be taxed at your marginal tax rate and if it is paid from a taxed source, you also receive a 15 per cent tax offset (tax-free for those 60 and over).

Once you start a pension or annuity a minimum amount, based on your age, is required to be paid to you each year. It is calculated as a percentage of your superannuation balance at 1 July each year as shown in table 6.4 (overleaf). There is no maximum amount other than the balance of your super account.

TABLE 6.4: minimum percentage age factors (2025–26)

Age	Minimum % withdrawal
Under 65	4
65–74	5
75–79	6
80–84	7
85–89	9
90–94	11
95 or more	14

Source: © Australian Taxation Office for the Commonwealth of Australia.

👆 TAX FACT

To be eligible for the Age Pension you must satisfy both the income and assets tests.

Income test

Senior Australians may be entitled to the full age pension if your income is less than $212 a fortnight as a single or $372 fortnightly as a couple. Deeming – rather than actuals – is used to calculate income from financial investments. The deeming rate is currently 0.25 per cent on the first $62 600 of financial assets owned by an individual or the first $103 800 by a couple. Above these thresholds, the deeming rate of return is 2.25 per cent.

Assets test

Single homeowners must have assets other than their home worth less than $314 000, rising to $470 000 for a home-owning couple. These thresholds increase by $252 000 for non-homeowners ($566 000 for singles and $722 000 for couples).

70 DEATH BENEFITS

Since superannuation became compulsory 33 years ago, retirement nest eggs have grown substantially and are an integral part of most estate planning. Premature death may mean a large payment to family members, particularly when a life insurance policy is attached to the fund.

> **♀ TIP**

Superannuation does not form part of your estate. If you don't put a 'binding nomination' in place, the trustee of your super fund has absolute discretion in distributing your super benefits to anyone they please.

To ensure that your super funds are properly dealt with upon your death, make a 'binding nomination' with the super fund trustee. Binding nominations must be witnessed by two independent individuals and expire every three years, so make sure that you always update them.

♦ TAX FACT

Unlike other countries, there is no inheritance tax in Australia. But don't be fooled because there are three things in life that are certain: taxes, death…and taxes on death!

If a death benefit is going to a dependant, such as a spouse or minor children, then it can be paid either as an income stream or as a lump-sum amount. Lump-sum payments to dependants are tax-free. However, a death benefit can only be paid as a lump sum to a non-dependant.

The popularity of superannuation as a low-tax environment within which to grow wealth, coupled with longer life expectancies, has resulted in an increasing number of financially independent people receiving a superannuation death benefit from a parent.

⚠ PITFALL

Lump-sum payments to non-dependants are taxed at 17 per cent on the taxed element while the untaxed element is taxed at a maximum rate of 32 per cent.

If you don't have a dependant to pay your death benefit to, there are a few strategies that you can use that can make a big difference to the final amount of tax payable. Accordingly, it is recommended that you discuss succession issues with a professional adviser.

If you are suffering from a terminal illness, you may want to consider withdrawing your entire super as a lump sum tax-free so that upon death it passes through your will to your independent family members tax-free as well.

Alternatively, consider withdrawing your super and then making non-concessional super contributions up to the non-concessional three-year bring forward limit so that any superannuation death benefit will comprise a tax-free element.

71 LOST OR UNCLAIMED SUPER

We work hard for our money, so it is surprising that so many people ignore one of their biggest assets: super. You should always keep track of your super by checking your annual statements for employer contributions, fees and insurance cover, and you should analyse fund performance in general.

Starting a new job can be exciting but also nerve-racking at the same time. The turnover in the Australian workforce is greater than ever, with the Australian Bureau of Statistics estimating that about 1.1 million people change jobs every year. If you do change your job, do not neglect your super. It can be very easy to forget it, particularly if you change both job and address, as you may not get statements in the future. It is wise to arrange for your super from past jobs to be rolled over into your new account.

> **♀TIP**
>
> You may have some lost super if you have changed your name (for example, through marriage), your address or your job. Ensure that you notify all of your super funds when you change address or you may risk losing touch with your funds.

Within your *myGov* account linked to the ATO you can click on 'Manage my super' to help you search for any lost and unclaimed super. You can also complete a paper form *Searching for lost and unclaimed super* (NAT 2476) and lodge with the ATO. Conversely you can call the ATO on 13 28 65 but you will need to supply your name, date of birth and TFN as well any details that you do have of your various super funds. Be prepared for a lengthy wait on the phone though.

> **♀TIP**
>
> Simply fill in an electronic form in the ATO section of the myGov website my.gov.au and arrange to consolidate lost superannuation accounts online.

If the ATO finds a match it will provide a list of all accounts on the lost members register (LMR) as well as any other unclaimed super amounts held by the ATO. Any lost super listed on the LMR is held by the relevant super funds.

Where an account is found on the LMR, you should:

- contact the super fund to update them with your personal details
- consolidate your super funds
- withdraw your benefit, if your account balance is less than $200 and certain criteria are met.

TAX FACT

Superannuation funds that hold more than one account for the same individual are required to consolidate those accounts where possible so that members do not have to pay unnecessary fees and other charges on multiple accounts.

TIP

If you have more than one super account, consider rolling them all into one super fund and save on fees as well as being able to manage your super more easily. Many funds make it easier for you by providing a 'consolidation' service, but make sure you check what your fund will charge you before you close the account and whether you'll lose any benefits.

TAX FACT

Since 2021, the ATO have consolidated superannuation accounts worth $6.4 billion.

TAX FACT

Lost or inactive superannuation accounts with balances under $6000 are transferred to the ATO. If you have a superannuation account balance of less than $6000 and it has been inactive but you want to keep it open then you can make a written declaration via the *Inactive low-balance accounts – Authorising your fund to provide a written declaration to the ATO* form (NAT 75198). Since 1 July 2013, the ATO has been paying interest on all lost super accounts reclaimed.

♀ TIP

The best advice that I can give about superannuation is to start at a young age, but sadly most people don't think about their retirement income until it is almost too late in life. The thought of superannuation may be dull and boring when you are 21, but it really is one of the best investment vehicles for your money. Money makes money so the quicker you can build up your nest egg, the less risk that you will need to take later in life. There are tax savings for salary sacrificing into super with as much as 32 per cent for those in the highest tax bracket. Most people will save at least $1700 in tax for every $10 000 sacrificed. That adds up over time.

♦ TAX FACT

Since 1 July 2017, individuals can make voluntary contributions into superannuation of up to $15 000 per year ($50 000 in total) to purchase a first home. These contributions are not in addition to the existing $30 000 contribution limit. Deemed earnings are calculated at the shortfall interest charge (currently 7.17 per cent). Withdrawals are taxed at marginal tax rates less a 30 per cent offset.

♦ TAX FACT

The maximum releasable amount of voluntary concessional and non-concessional contributions under the First Home Super Saver Scheme is $50 000.

♦ TAX FACT

Under the Help to Buy Scheme, the federal government will make a contribution of 30 per cent for an existing home (or 40 per cent for a new home) in exchange for a share interest. The scheme is available for those wishing to buy their first property to live in with eligible individuals having a yearly income under $100 000 or couples or single parents with income under $160 000. Buyers will be required to have a deposit of at least 2 per cent, manage all other associated costs (such as stamp duty, legal and bank fees) and be able to finance the remainder through a participating lender. Region-specific property price caps also apply ranging from $500 000 in regional South Australia to $1 300 000 in Sydney.

PART VII
YOUR BUSINESS

There comes a time in everyone's life when you think—even for just one moment—about running your own business. As a business owner myself I can tell you that running a business is gratifying and can offer you many rewards and benefits. But it brings with it quite a few nightmares along the way.

Before you get too caught up in complicated tax structures and tax planning, the first thing you must consider is whether you are actually running a business or merely practising a hobby. The nature of your trading activity will largely determine if you are running a business or not. The ATO generally looks at trading volume as the key indicator for determining any tax implications.

The past decade has seen an increase in the number of people who are selling online on a full-time basis. If you are selling a few old bits and pieces from around the house that you no longer use, the ATO sees this activity as merely a 'hobby' and the income is not assessable. But if you start selling new items as well as actively trading second-hand 'bargains' that you pick up along the way, the ATO views you as 'being in business' and any profits that you derive as being assessable.

♀ TIP

If you are considering buying an existing business then ensure that you conduct a thorough due diligence so that you are buying the business assets but not any surprises. The purchase of a business is full of untold opportunities but also unknown problems with potential skeletons hiding in the closet.

Part VII is designed to help you stay in control of your tax affairs during the various stages of your business. Tax is the biggest expense that a business will encounter. As your business grows and changes, so will your tax situation. There will be additional tax obligations such as how to pay employees and other businesses and how to report and pay tax and superannuation.

⏺ TAX FACT

When starting a business, the most common tax registrations needed include the following:

- a TFN (not required for sole traders as you use your existing TFN)
- an Australian business number (ABN)
- goods and services tax (GST)
- PAYG withholding.

♀ TIP

When you start a new business, take advantage of the multitude of free services supported by different government departments to assist businesses in areas such as planning, marketing, budgeting, cash flow and networking. There are also a number of different grants available. See www.business.gov.au for more information.

🎁 BONUS RESOURCES

For more information on running a small business, the ATO has an excellent publication called *Tax basics for small business* (NAT 1908).

72 CHOOSING THE RIGHT BUSINESS STRUCTURE

If you are planning to make a fortune, perhaps you should consider your business structure before you give away half of it in taxes.

The structure of a business will affect:

- how much tax your business has to pay
- how other businesses deal with you
- your administration costs
- your level of asset protection.

The most common structures used by Australian businesses are:

- sole traders
- partnerships
- companies
- trusts.

Sole traders

Sole traders are taxed in exactly the same way as individuals. A business enjoying good profits can expect to pay tax at the higher marginal rates. There is no asset protection if you are a sole trader so beware of 'creditors and predators'.

Partnerships

Partnerships are often preferred by husband–and–wife businesses and also where personal services are provided. They have a simple and cost–effective structure, but their major disadvantage is that they offer no asset protection due to unlimited liability. Partnerships do not pay tax in their own right. Instead, each partner pays tax on their share of the net partnership income at their marginal tax rate.

Companies

A private company (with 'Pty Ltd' at the end of the business name) is the most common business structure for operating entities, particularly where capital gains are not likely and where the small business capital gains tax concessions will not apply. Unlike sole traders and partnerships, companies have limited liability, although personal guarantees may be required by directors from time to time. As table 7.1 shows, the corporate tax rate is a flat 30 per cent, but reduced to 25 percent for small/medium companies (with turnover under $50 million). In addition to the under $50 million threshold requirement, the companies will only get the lower 25 per cent company tax rate applied to their taxable income if their passive income (such as interest income, rent, royalties, dividend income and net capital gains) constitutes less than 80 per cent of their assessable income.

TABLE 7.1: tax rates for companies (2024–25)

Annual turnover threshold	Tax for entities under threshold	Tax for other corporate entities
$50 million	25%	30%

Source: © Australian Taxation Office for the Commonwealth of Australia.

♀TIP

Careful tax planning is required for companies near the $50 million threshold level as an error could cost $500 000 extra tax (5 per cent) for those working on a 20 per cent net profit margin.

⚠ PITFALL

Loans (or debts forgiven) by private companies to their shareholders are generally treated by the ATO as unfranked dividends assessable in the individual shareholder's income tax return. To avoid this, there needs to be a loan agreement in place between the company and the shareholder. The terms must include principal and interest repayments, over a maximum of seven years. The interest rate charged on the loan must be based on the benchmark interest rate set by the ATO at the end of each financial year (8.77 per cent for 2024–25 year).

⚠ PITFALL

Vehicles purchased through a company or trust structure may be subject to fringe benefits tax.

Trusts

Using a family trust is an excellent way to minimise the overall income tax liability for a business. A trust can also help with managing assets and liabilities, as well as offering flexibility for estate-planning purposes.

☝ TAX FACT

After enjoying strong growth at the start of the 21st century, popularity of trusts in Australia is waning. In the 2021–22 financial year there were just over 986 000 trusts which lodged a tax return.

Family trusts are not directly taxed. Instead it is the beneficiaries of the trust who are subject to income tax on their share of the trust's net income. Beneficiaries also have the ability to obtain the full benefit of any small business capital gains tax concessions and franking credits.

A company is often used to act as a corporate trustee of a trust so that the personal assets of the business owners have some form of protection from any future claims made against the entity.

Where partners are likely to be admitted, the business could be run through a unit trust with the respective units being held by a family trust.

⚲ TIP

If a business, via a family trust, is deriving substantial income and all of the individuals are on marginal tax rates in excess of the corporate tax rate, consider establishing a corporate beneficiary to limit the overall tax payable.

⚠ PITFALL

Trustees of a discretionary trust will be assessed on 47 per cent of the trust income if they do not document their resolution for distribution of income before 30 June each year. The trust's accounts do not need to be prepared at this time.

⚠ PITFALL

In December 2022, the ATO issued Taxation Ruling *TR 2022/4* and Practical Compliance Guideline *PCG 2022/2* on how the current trust distribution laws under s100A should operate as they are overtly concerned about the use of discretionary trusts as tax minimisation vehicles. s100A is an anti-avoidance rule that could result in the ATO looking through arrangements and assessing income to the trustee at 47 per cent. Given the potential severity of non-compliance with s100A, it would be prudent to take a conservative view by avoiding any circular flow of funds and engaging a registered tax agent who is proficient on the topic.

🖋 TAX FACT

While restructuring costs (income tax, stamp duty and legal fees) can be expensive if you don't pick the right structure upfront, professional expenses incurred in relation to the establishment of a new business are deductible in full. CGT rollover relief is also available for small businesses to change their legal structure without attracting CGT.

73 TAX OBLIGATIONS

Most business owners will tell you that they hate it, but one of the most important tasks in running a business is meeting your tax obligations. These include collecting and reporting GST, lodging business activity statements (BAS) and submitting an annual tax return.

GST

If your business has a gross business income (GST turnover) of $75 000 or more ($150 000 or more if it is a nonprofit organisation) or provides taxi travel, you will need to:

- register for GST
- charge 10 per cent GST on the price of a taxable supply
- issue tax invoices (for amounts greater than $75) to customers, showing your ABN
- report and remit GST charged on the taxable supplies to the ATO in the required instalments:
    - monthly (if turnover is *greater* than $20 million)
    - quarterly (if turnover is *less* than $20 million).

Small businesses (where turnover is less than $10 million) use the cash method of reporting, while all other businesses must use the accrual method.

GST is calculated from the GST-inclusive price as follows:

$$GST = GST\text{-inclusive price} \div 11$$

> ♀ **TIP**
>
> If your business is struggling for cashflow, consider changing its GST reporting cycle to monthly reporting so that you can get quicker access to the GST refunds that you are entitled to. If you do elect to change the reporting cycle, please note that you must keep reporting in this manner for at least 12 months before you can revert back to your old cycle again.

> ♀ **TIP**
>
> Be disciplined and keep at least one-third of the income you receive aside to cover your GST and income tax obligations.

If your business does not quote its ABN, then your payer may deduct 47 per cent withholding tax from payment.

The purchaser (rather than the seller) of new residential premises is required to lodge and pay GST. The seller still reports the sale in their monthly or quarterly BAS but will receive a credit for the payment submitted by the purchaser.

Activity statements

Businesses are required to complete an activity statement to report and pay a number of tax obligations, such as GST, PAYG instalments, PAYG withholding and fringe benefits tax (FBT).

All businesses registered for GST need to regularly lodge a BAS with the ATO on either a monthly (21 days after period end), quarterly (28 October, 28 February, 28 April and 28 July) or annual basis (before lodgement due date for income tax return). Any GST paid on purchases is offset against the GST collected from customers. The net amount is remitted to the ATO via your BAS.

Common GST mistakes include:

- claiming GST credits on bank fees and government charges where no GST has been charged in the first place
- not remitting GST on government grants and incentives that were received inclusive of GST
- incorrectly claiming GST credits on GST-free purchases such as basic food items, exports and some health services
- claiming the entire GST credit on a car purchased for more than the luxury car limit of $80 567 GST-inclusive (increasing to $91 387 for fuel efficient vehicles)
- not apportioning private usage for expenses that have GST charged.

Large entities—those with a turnover of $20 million or more—are required to make PAYG income tax instalments monthly, rather than quarterly.

👆 TAX FACT

If you receive cryptocurrency for goods or services you provide as part of your business, you need to include the value of the cryptocurrency in Australian dollars as part of your ordinary income. This is the same process as receiving any other non-cash consideration under a barter transaction.

? FAQ

I'm about to get a car under my company and will be using it approximately 70 per cent for work and 30 per cent personal. In order to avoid FBT I will pay for my personal expenses incurred. Do I still need to register for FBT?

Yes you will still need to register for FBT and submit an FBT return each year, even if the net FBT payable is zero because you made a personal contribution.

💡 TIP

If you want to manage your business tax affairs online with the ATO, there is a Business Portal available on the ATO website bp.ato.gov.au. It is safe to use as your information is protected by online security credentials. You must download the myGovID app on your smart device (which is different to your myGov account) and then establish your authorisations using the Relationship Authorisation Manager (info.authorisationmanager.gov.au) in order to use it on your computer. You can view your statement of account, update contact details, and prepare and lodge activity statements.

👆 TAX FACT

In 2023–24, the ATO conducted over 2650 reviews and audits into phoenix schemes and raised liabilities and cash collections of $412 million. The ATO also raised $2.1 billion as part of its Shadow Economy program and a further $5.7 billion from the Tax Avoidance Taskforce.

74 RECORD KEEPING

While it is a legal requirement that you keep business records for tax purposes, it is also a good idea to keep excellent records in order to maximise your income tax return claims.

> **⚠ PITFALL**
>
> If you do not keep proper records, the ATO can impose a penalty of up to $6600.

Excellent record-keeping practices include:

- maintaining a cashbook (either manually or electronically) to record all information from your bank account
- keeping adequate employment records, including:
  - PAYG payment summaries
  - employment termination payments
  - reportable fringe benefits.
- keeping all documents in a safe and secure place for a period of five years
- fulfilling tax obligations such as:
  - withholding PAYG tax
  - recording all GST obligations
  - paying superannuation contributions to complying superannuation funds.

The following is a quick checklist of the ATO requirements relating to record keeping.

Records relating to payments to employees:

- employee payment records
- employee termination payment summaries
- fringe benefits provided to employees
- PAYG payment summaries
- superannuation records

- TFN declarations
- withholding variation notices.

Records relating to income tax and GST:

- sales records:
  - bank statements
  - cash register tapes
  - credit card statements
  - deposit books
  - tax invoices.
- purchase and expense records:
  - bank statements
  - chequebook butts
  - credit card statements
  - logbooks showing any private use
  - tax invoices.
- year-end income tax records:
  - capital gains tax records
  - depreciation schedules
  - list of debtors
  - list of creditors
  - stocktake records.

PAYG withholding records relating to business payments:

- amounts withheld from payments where no ABN was quoted
- PAYG withholding voluntary agreements.

75 DEFERRING TAX

We all have to pay our fair share of taxes but if you can legitimately delay the inevitable to another tax year then you should do so. Any deferral of taxes will help cash flow as you potentially get a further 12 months before you need to pay the tax man. Tax rates may also be lower in subsequent years.

Delaying the derivation of income and bringing forward deductions are the two main ways of deferring your taxable income to the next financial year.

Deferring income

In order to work out the best way to defer assessable income to future years, you need to know how the ATO will assess your business income in the first place.

Most small businesses will be assessed on a cash basis where income is recognised only when cash is received. Constructive receipt is important here so it is possible to minimise income by deferring receipts until after 1 July.

Larger businesses will need to use the accruals basis where income is recognised as it is earned and not as money is received. If your business operates on an accruals basis you may want to defer your invoicing until next tax year.

Maximise deductions

If you have annual expenses such as subscriptions and insurance due in July, pay them before 30 June to reduce this year's tax. As a small business, you can use the prepayments concession where you can claim a deduction for the total expense you prepaid if you receive the goods or services in full within 12 months. Other deductible expenses to scrutinise include bad debts, depreciation on business assets, revaluing your trading stock and making superannuation contributions before year end.

You do not need to actually have paid out any money to have 'incurred' a loss or outgoing. If you are definitively committed, or have completely subjected yourself to the expenditure, it will be deductible. Mere provisions, such as for annual leave and long-service leave, are not deductible because the employer is not definitively committed to the expenditure.

⚨ TIP

If you pay annual staff bonuses after year end, pass a resolution before 30 June and have it in writing that you are committed to the expenditure in order for it to be tax-deductible this year.

76 TRADING STOCK

The ATO defines trading stock as anything you produce, manufacture, acquire or purchase for manufacture, sale or exchange in your business, including livestock.

If the value of your trading stock at the end of the income year is:

- more than at the start of the financial year—the difference is added to your assessable income
- less than at the start of the financial year—a deduction can be claimed for the difference.

Small businesses only need to make an adjustment to their taxable income if their closing stock varies by more than $5000 from their opening stock figure.

An annual stocktake is usually conducted by businesses, generally as close as possible to the end of the financial year, to determine the value of trading stock on hand at 30 June.

If you run a business that sells food and you take an item for private use, such as milk or a meal, you must account for it as if you had sold it and include the value of the item in your assessable income. Owners can either keep a tab of the actual value of items used for private purposes or apply a standard amount from the ATO for your industry.

👍 TAX FACT

Taxation Determination TD 2024/8 provides the amount that the ATO will accept as estimates for the value of goods taken from trading stock for private use by taxpayers in different industries. Amounts range from $1040 per adult per annum for a butcher to $5420 per adult per annum for a mixed business.

Irrespective of how they are valued for accounting purposes, there are only three methods allowed for valuing your trading stock for tax purposes:

- cost
- market selling value
- replacement value.

💡 TIP

The best stock valuation method to adopt is the method that produces the lowest value of trading stock. If you have different classes of stock then you can use a different basis of valuation for each class as well as for each individual item of stock, although these calculations can get messy.

You can change the method used each year so long as the opening stock figure is the same as the closing stock figure from the previous year.

💡 TIP

If you have some old plant or stock that your business simply can't sell, consider physically writing it off before 30 June and get a tax deduction for it this year.

77 BAD DEBTS

One of the things you invariably have to deal with when you are in business is customers who won't pay for your goods or services. Some customers don't have the cash flow to pay, while some will dispute the debt. And then there are those who are simply bad eggs and have no intention whatsoever of paying you.

Most businesses are required to record their income on an accruals basis for tax purposes. This means that they are required to show all sales as taxable income even if they don't receive the cash!

Some debts owed to a business can be quite sizeable, so having to pay tax on income not received can have a significant impact on cash flow. Luckily, the ATO allows a deduction for bad debts, but certain criteria must be satisfied.

Like obsolete stock, the ATO will only grant an income tax deduction for your business for a bad debt if:

- there was a debt in existence
- the debt was physically written off prior to 30 June
- the debt was genuinely bad by the terms of agreement or other reasonable criteria
- the debt was originally shown as income in the current or a previous financial year.

⚠ PITFALL

If businesses do not physically write off a debt before 30 June they are not entitled to a tax deduction in that financial year.

As the criteria require action by the business, namely writing off the debt, a review of all debts by a company before 30 June each year is crucial.

Most business owners get confused with deductions for bad debts and why there should be a nil impact for tax purposes when they have outlaid money for the goods and services in the first place. What they don't take into account is that they are already getting deductions for their costs (such as rent, wages and materials) incurred in the production of the goods.

Unfortunately, having to write off bad debts is simply a cost of running your own business. But make sure that you do so in a timely manner.

78 HOME-BASED BUSINESSES

Starting up a home-based business can be one of the most rewarding things that you can do. Most businesses, mine included, originally started from home. There are many benefits to working from home, including flexibility, saving on travel time and getting some extra tax deductions. There is also a bonus in not paying any extra rent.

You may be able to claim the business-related portion of the following 'running' costs:

- depreciation of home-office furniture, fittings and equipment such as computers and desks (certain items can be claimed in full by small businesses that choose the instant asset write-off method—see tip 82 for more information).
- heating, cooling and lighting
- home telephone
- internet access
- printer and printer cartridges
- repairs to your home-office furniture and fittings
- stationery.

⚠ PITFALL

If you run your business from your own home, there is a possibility that your home could be subject to capital gains tax. Make sure you consult a tax adviser about your own particular circumstances. Sometimes it may be cheaper to pay for separate office space rather than incur a big tax bill in the future.

The ATO is quite particular with the claiming of home-office 'occupancy' expenses. If you genuinely operate a business from your home you are allowed to claim a proportion of mortgage interest or rent based on the actual floor space that you use for the business.

✋ TAX FACT

If your home is your place of business, you can also claim a deduction for your occupancy expenses including:

- council rates
- home-insurance premiums
- mortgage interest
- rent.

The ATO looks at a number of factors to determine if your home is your place of business. The area must be:

- clearly identifiable as a place of business
- not readily suitable for use for private purposes
- used almost exclusively for business purposes
- used regularly for visits by clients or customers.

Home office deductions are usually calculated as follows:

Floor area used × relevant expenditure ÷ total floor area

✎ EXAMPLE

If your home office is 6 m × 3 m (that is, 18 square metres) and the total house is 100 square metres in size, you can claim 18 per cent of your occupancy costs for income tax purposes.

⚠ PITFALL

The ATO considers that any initial website development costs are capital in nature and only deductible over five years. However, website running costs (such as the annual domain name registration, site hosting, ongoing content and technical maintenance) are deemed to be operating costs that are claimable in the year that they are incurred.

♡ TIP

If the ATO conducts an audit into your business affairs, it will not accept estimates, so you must be quite accurate with your calculations. I recommend getting your measuring tape out and writing down the dimensions of your office and your overall house. I find it also helps to strengthen your case if you take photos of your office, especially if you move house down the track.

79 SHARING ECONOMY

The last five years have seen a surge of the sharing economy with Uber, GoCatch, Airbnb, Stayz, Spacer, Camplify, Car Next Door, HomeKey,

GoCatch and Airtasker just to name a few who have become household names, not just in Australia but right across the globe.

Not only are we becoming trusted users of these services, more and more people (if my mates are any guides) are themselves offering these services and picking up a bit of extra money for the household each week on top of their normal salary. What is really important is that if you provide goods or services through any of these apps or websites, you have tax obligations with all payments you receive through the sharing economy being subject to income tax after allowing for deductions for associated expenses.

You will be considered to be operating a business which will require an ABN and you must declare the income in the business income section in your tax return.

> 👆 **TAX FACT**

> Assessable income from the sharing economy may include:
> - income earned from performing services for a fee
> - ride-sourcing services for a fare (considered a taxi travel service for GST purposes)
> - food delivery
> - tasking or other odd jobs arranged through a sharing economy platform
> - renting out a room or a whole property that you own or lease (such as your home, a rental property or a parking space) for a short-time basis
> - income from sharing other forms of property, such as a motor vehicle or caravan.

If your turnover is over $75 000 per year, you may be required to register for GST and lodge quarterly business activity statements.

While there is no GST on residential rent, all ride-sourcing enterprises must have an ABN and be registered for GST regardless of turnover.

⚠ PITFALL

If you rent out a parking space, you may need to pay CGT when you eventually sell it or property it's attached to. A small bit of income now may lead to large unexpected tax liability in the future.

You can claim income tax deductions relating to income you earn but if your expenses are for both business and private use, you can only claim a deduction for the business-related portion. Any fees or commissions charged by a sharing economy facilitator can be claimed as a deduction.

♀ TIP

If you are concerned you might get a tax bill because you think your business will generate a profit, you can choose to make a prepayment of tax rather than wait for the nasty tax bill at the end of the year. This voluntary payment made in advance can be made at any time and as often as you like to make it easier for you to manage your tax.

? FAQ

I am thinking about letting out a room for a night here and there to travellers via one of those online sites such as Airbnb. Would I need to declare the money received as income? What are the implications, if any, if I don't declare it?

The tax rules are pretty clear. Any rental income that you receive — no matter how small — needs to be declared as assessable income in your return and you'll need to pay tax on it.

Trying to dodge the tax office by not declaring the income will end in tears. You may think that the income is so little that the ATO won't bother, but the cash economy is huge and is definitely on the tax man's hit list. Something like this is advertised on the internet so the ATO is more likely to find out about it. Guests are paying electronically, which makes it easier to track down. I should also warn that people renting rooms in their home also need to be aware it's probably opening them up to capital gains tax when they sell their homes down the track.

80 EMPLOYING PEOPLE

So you took the first step and started your own business. Now business has gone crazy and sales are through the roof and you need to hire someone else to help you in handling the growth.

While it is always exciting when a small business starts to grow and you need to employ staff for the first time, you need to be aware of some of the obligations that come with being an employer. Non-compliance could lead to penalties, which include fines and prosecution.

Wages and conditions

All issues concerning wages and employment conditions in the private sector fall under the *Fair Work Act 2009*, which requires you to maintain a minimum standard of pay, conditions and entitlements for your employees. There are 12 National Employment Standards that apply to all employers and employees.

📢 PROPOSED CHANGE

The 2025–26 federal budget proposed the banning of non-compete clauses in employment contracts for workers earning less than the high income threshold in the *Fair Work Act* (currently $175000) from 2027.

Employment records

You must issue pay slips to each employee and keep accurate and complete time and wages records for a minimum of seven years.

Taxation obligations

Your taxation obligations include:

- registering with the ATO as a new employer
- obtaining *TFN declarations* (NAT 3092) from employees
- report tax withheld and superannuation information to the ATO through Single Touch Payroll

- withholding PAYG tax from payments you make to your employees and paying it to the ATO
- preparing year-end PAYG payment summaries for employees
- calculating any employment termination payments
- paying fringe benefits tax for benefits paid to employees
- paying payroll tax if total wages exceed the exemption threshold applicable in your state or territory:
  - ACT: 6.85 per cent over $2 000 000
  - NSW: 5.45 per cent over $1 200 000
  - Northern Territory: 5.5 per cent over $1 500 000
  - Queensland: 4.75 per cent over $1 300 000
  - South Australia: 4.95 per cent over $1 500 000
  - Tasmania: 4 per cent over $1 250 000
  - Victoria: 4.85 per cent over $1 000 000
  - Western Australia: 5.5 per cent over $1 000 000

♀ TIP

While they need to be provided by 14 July, your employees will appreciate it if you finalise their annual PAYG payment summary as soon as possible after year end so they can complete their own tax returns.

♦ TAX FACT

Employers must report tax and super information to the ATO through Single Touch Payroll which is available through most payroll, accounting and business management software.

Superannuation obligations

Employing people, whether full time, part time or casual, will trigger the superannuation guarantee legislation which requires you to pay a minimum of 12 per cent of the earnings base (generally ordinary time earnings) into employees' choice of super fund, via *SuperStream*, within 28 days after the end of the quarter.

Holiday and leave entitlements

You need to pay public holidays for all employees except for those who are only paid for hours worked such as contract workers and casual employees. Other paid leave should include annual, sick and long-service leave.

Other employment issues to consider include:

- anti–discrimination
- equal employment opportunity
- occupational health and safety legislation
- public liability insurance
- workers compensation.

81 SINGLE TOUCH PAYROLL

I do not consider myself that old but when I first started doing the weekly payroll for companies I did it manually via the old Zions wage books. After working out everyone's net pay, I used to write a cheque monthly to the ATO for the tax withheld on employees' wages. And at year end I would hand-write the group certificates (now known as PAYG Payment Summaries) for every employee and then cross check the whole year's calculations with my trusty calculator.

So, it is with a happy accountant's heart that we are in the digital era of today with technology making it so much easier for us bean counters! Not only has accounting software such as Xero, MYOB and QuickBooks made it simpler to run a business, the government has also moved with the times as well by aligning their reporting to the digital world.

One of those changes is Single Touch Payroll (STP) which is a relatively new system of reporting employee payroll information such as gross wages, superannuation and PAYG withheld each time you pay them. It started for larger employers from 1 July 2018 and a year later for those businesses with 19 or less employees. Since 1 July 2020, closely held payees—someone who is directly related to the entity (such as family members, directors or shareholders)—have needed to report through STP. Since 1 January 2022 STP was expanded to collect additional payroll information.

> **♀ TIP**
>
> To make STP reporting as simple as possible for your business, regularly check your payroll systems to ensure that you are paying your employees and their entitlements correctly and addressing any overpayments in a timely manner. Also make sure that you maintain accurate information for employees including names, addresses and date of birth records.

Using payroll software, or another solution that is STP ready, you do not need to modify your pay cycle so you can continue to pay your employees weekly, fortnightly or monthly and it doesn't matter if you pay employees on different days of the week either. You also no longer need to give your employees a payment summary or income statement as the information you report and finalise through STP will be available to your employees on their respective myGov accounts automatically.

> **♀ TIP**
>
> If you already use accounting or payroll software, talk to your provider and they will tell you which of their products offer STP. Otherwise ask your accountant or bookkeeper for their recommendations. Failing that the STP Product Register (softwaredevelopers.ato.gov.au/product-register) provides a list of over 400 commercially available STP products, which have met the security requirements under the Digital Service Provider (DSP) Operational Framework. All products included in the register can generate an STP compliant file, which can be sent directly from your payroll software to the ATO.

There will be a need to confirm your STP information at the end of the financial year to ensure that the data you have been reporting throughout the year to the ATO is complete and so your employees can then complete their tax returns. If you make a mistake, you will be able to make corrections.

👍 TAX FACT

Employees no longer get a payment summary or income statement but they can find the information needed to complete their tax return via ATO Online accessed through their myGov account. Any employee who does not have a myGov account can easily create one using an email address and password. Each time you pay an employee and report through STP, their year-to-date tax and super information will be updated in myGov. The ATO has an informative factsheet to help your employees understand this change on their website www.ato.gov. au/business/single-touch-payroll/single-touch-payroll-for-employees/what-stp-means-for-employees/

🎁 BONUS RESOURCES

For more detailed requirements of STP, including what you need to report, how to make corrections and finalising your STP data you can see the ATO's STP employer reporting guidelines on their website www.ato.gov.au/stp.

---

82 TAX CONCESSIONS AND OFFSETS

Small businesses have access to a range of concessions to help reduce their taxable income, designed to make tax administration easier. For example, they are entitled to immediate tax deductions for business expenses prepaid for 12 months in advance, such as interest.

Simplified depreciation rules

Businesses with an annual turnover under $10 million can immediately write off many depreciating assets that cost less than $1000 (reduced from $20 000 on 1 July 2025) exclusive of GST. For businesses that are registered for GST, the effective ticket-price threshold is $1099 as you can claim the 10 per cent GST rebate in your quarterly business activity statement.

> **⚠ PITFALL**
>
> The temporary full expensing measures that allowed the immediate write-off of new asset purchases ceased on 30 June 2023. Businesses must now revert back to the traditional depreciation of assets over their useful life, except for those that qualify for the instant asset write-off.

Small businesses can consolidate other assets above the instant asset write-off threshold (currently $1000) in a general small business pool at a rate of 15 per cent in the first income year and 30 per cent each income year after that.

Restart wage subsidy

Employers can receive up to $10 000 (GST inclusive) in government assistance if they hire a full-time job seeker aged 50 or older under the Restart wage subsidy program. Eligible employers will receive the payment if the job seeker was previously unemployed for a period of 6 months and subsequently employed for a minimum average of 20 hours per week.

> **📢 PROPOSED CHANGE**
>
> The 2025–26 federal budget proposed that small businesses will receive a $150 rebate on their energy bills from 1 July 2025.

> **⚠ PITFALL**
>
> The loss carry back tax offset that allowed companies to claim back tax paid in prior tax returns ceased on 30 June 2023. Businesses must now carry forward tax losses to offset profits made in future tax years.

Youth bonus wage subsidy

Eligible employers can receive up to $10 000 (GST inclusive) via the youth bonus wage subsidy if they hire a job seeker between 15 and 24 for a minimum average of 20 hours per week over six months.

Since 1 July 2022, a 30 per cent refundable digital games tax offset of up to $20 million per annum is available for eligible Australian development expenditure. Games must not have gambling elements and eligible companies must have incurred a minimum of $500 000 qualifying Australian games expenditure.

Other wage subsidies

Eligible employers can receive up to $6500 (GST inclusive) if they hire the following job seekers for a minimum average of 20 hours per week over six months:

- youth wage subsidy—job seekers who are between 25 and 29 years of age

- parents wage subsidy—a job seeker who is a principal carer parent

- long-term unemployed subsidy—a long-term unemployed job seeker who has been registered with employment services for 12 months

- indigenous wage subsidy—an indigenous job seeker who has been registered with employment services for six months.

Income averaging

Primary producers and special professionals (such as authors, inventors, performing artists, production associates and sportspersons) may have their income averaged out over a number of years to smooth out any unexpected high increases in tax due to the abnormal levels of income that are derived in one financial year.

Export Market Development Grant

Since 1 July 2021, small and medium-sized businesses with annual turnover under $20 million have been able to receive government assistance via the Export Market Development Grants (EMDG) scheme on developing export markets. Administered by Austrade,

SMEs with turnover under $20 million can apply for grants for one or two years as follows:

- tier 1—for eligible SMEs new to exporting
- tier 2—for eligible exporters planning on expanding their presence in current markets or enter new markets
- tier 3—for eligible exporters who are planning a strategic shift in their exporting business.

⚠ PITFALL

> The Export Market Development Grant Program is temporarily closed. Round 5 of the Program is likely to open in early 2026.

Fuel tax credits

Businesses can claim a credit for the fuel tax (excise or customs duty) that's included in the price of fuel used in:

- machinery
- plant
- equipment
- heavy vehicles
- light vehicles travelling off public roads or on private roads.

The rates of credit for fuel acquired range from 32.4 cents per litre for liquid fuels used by heavy vehicles travelling on public roads up to 50.8 cents per litre for fuels used for other business uses.

Australian Apprenticeships Incentive System

Since 1 July 2022, employers who offer apprenticeship opportunities in occupations on the Australian Apprenticeship Priority List (including, but not limited to, arborists, bakers/chefs/cooks, carpenters/joiners/cabinetmakers, bricklayers/stonemasons, electricians, gardeners, hairdressers, plumbers and tilers) may be eligible for a hiring incentive of up to $5000 in the first year of the apprenticeship.

Under the system, an Australian apprentice undertaking a qualification at either Certificate III, IV, Diploma or Advanced Diploma level leading to an occupation on the Australian Apprenticeships Priority List may be eligible for an Apprentice Training Support Payment of up to $5000 for the first two years of their Australian Apprenticeship.

📢 PROPOSED CHANGE

The 2025–26 federal budget proposed a financial incentive of up to $10 000 to eligible apprentices in housing construction occupations from 1 July 2025.

Research and development tax incentive

If your business is involved in research and development (R&D) in Australia to create new or improved materials, devices, processes, products or services it may be eligible for an R&D tax incentive. The Department of Industry, Science and Research defines R&D activity as systematic, investigative and experimental activity that:

- involves both innovation and high levels of technical risk
- is for the process of producing new knowledge or improvements.

The R&D tax incentive is a 43.5 per cent refundable tax offset for companies with an annual turnover less than $20 million.

Other eligible companies with a higher turnover are eligible for a 38.5 per cent non-refundable tax offset for R&D expenditure up to 2 per cent of total expenditure. This increases to 46.5 per cent when R&D expenditure is more than 2 per cent of total expenditure. However, since 1 July 2014, large businesses with annual Australian R&D claims in excess of $100 million are limited in receiving the R&D tax incentive to that amount, but will be eligible to claim the excess R&D expenditure as a general deduction. The ATO looks after this incentive jointly with AusIndustry. In order to be eligible you need to register each income year with the Industry Innovation and Science Australia Board and meet the minimum R&D threshold expenditure of $20 000.

Hydrogen production tax incentive

The hydrogen production tax incentive is a refundable tax offset of $2 per kilogram of renewable hydrogen produced in Australia. The incentive is available for up to ten years per project between 2027–28 and 2039–40. Eligible entities must be corporations (that is, trusts and partnerships are not entitled to the offset). Eligible hydrogen must be produced under a production profile certified by the Clean Energy Regulator (who jointly administers the tax offset with the ATO) and subject of a registered Product Guarantee of Origin certificate.

Critical minerals production tax incentive

The critical minerals production tax offset is valued at 10 per cent of relevant processing and refining costs — excluding capital and financing expenditure — for the 31 minerals on the Australian critical minerals list. The incentive is available for up to ten years per project between 2027–28 and 2039–40. Eligible companies must register with the Department of Industry, Science and Resources who jointly administers the tax offset with the ATO.

83 SELLING OR CLOSING DOWN

If you close down or sell your business, there are significant opportunities to do some tax planning and minimise CGT as much as possible.

If you are a retiring small business owner you may be entitled to disregard some or all of your capital gains if you:

- are 55 years or over
- retired or are permanently incapacitated
- owned your 'small business CGT assets' for 15 years or more.

If you do not satisfy the above criteria, the ATO says you may still be entitled to the following concessions to reduce any potential taxable capital gain from the sale of your small business:

- 50 per cent general CGT discount—for capital gains on assets that you have held for 12 months or more
- small business 50 per cent active asset reduction—reduces the capital gains on 'active assets' by 50 per cent
- small business retirement exemption—disregards any remaining capital gain by up to a lifetime limit of $500 000 per individual if paid into a complying superannuation fund
- small business asset rollover—defers a capital gain where you acquire 'replacement assets'.

To qualify for these small business concessions, the ATO says you must satisfy the following conditions:

- You have been carrying on a business with a turnover under $2 million.
- The net value of your CGT assets and any related entities is a maximum of $6 million.
- Your CGT asset is an 'active asset'.
- If the asset is a share or interest in a trust:
  - there must be a 'controlling individual' just before the CGT event
  - the entity claiming the concession must be a 'CGT concession stakeholder' in the company.

⚠ PITFALL

If you use your home as a business office it is incorrect to think that if you don't claim 'occupancy' expenses (such as a portion of the mortgage interest, insurance and council rates) you are not liable for CGT.

The law clearly states that CGT is payable on the portion of the home used for running the business when:

- the home was acquired after 19 September 1985
- part of it was used to produce income at some time when it was owned
- the taxpayer would be entitled to deduct interest had it been incurred on money borrowed to buy the home.

When doing capital gains tax calculations on your home used for a business, the ATO allows you to have acquired it for its market value on the day when the property was first used to produce assessable income.

> **🎁 BONUS RESOURCES**
>
> For more information on how business sales are treated for CGT purposes, the ATO has an excellent *Guide to capital gains tax concessions for small business* (NAT 8384).

> **👍 TAX FACT**
>
> In addition to the four small business CGT concessions, there is a small business restructure rollover allowing the transfer of active assets — including CGT assets — from one entity to another, on or after 1 July 2016, without incurring an income tax liability. You can access this concession if your aggregated turnover is less than $10 million.

84 PERSONAL SERVICES INCOME

If you are a contractor or a consultant and you operate your business via a partnership, company or trust, you need to ensure that you satisfy the personal services income (PSI) rules, as you run the risk of being personally liable for tax on the income regardless of your business structure. The rules can also deny deductions for some business-related expenses incurred as a contractor.

If the majority of your income is for labour rather than for materials supplied or tools and equipment used to complete the job, then you will be subject to the PSI rules.

There is an exemption from the PSI rules if you pass the results test, which is a test to work out if you've received the income after achieving a specific result or outcome.

The maximum term allowed under Division 7A for most loan agreements is seven years unless the loan is secured by a mortgage over real property. In this instance, the maximum term for the loan can be 25 years but the market value of the property (less liabilities secured over the property in priority to the loan) must be at least 110 per cent of the amount of the loan. A written agreement can be drafted to cover loans which will be made to a shareholder or their associate for several income years in the future.

The minimum annual loan repayment of principal and interest required can be calculated each year as follows:

$$MYR\frac{(PI)}{1-\left(\dfrac{1}{1\,I}\right)^{T}}$$

Where:
MYR = minimum yearly repayment
P = amount of loan not repaid by the end of the previous income year
I = current year's benchmark interest rate
T = remaining loan term (in years)

> **⚠ PITFALL**
>
> Amounts treated as dividends under Division 7A are generally not frankable, even though they are taken to be paid out of the private company's profits. This will result in the undesirable situation of a potential double taxation of those earnings at both the company tax rate and the shareholder's personal tax rates.

87 FRANCHISING

If your business becomes quite successful you may toy with the thought of franchising it so that other people can pay you copious amounts of cash for your idea. Sounds really good in theory but you need excellent systems, patience and time to set it up properly.

Franchising is a highly complicated area with huge scope for franchisors to be sued by franchisees if you don't comply with the franchising laws correctly. It is strongly recommended that you hire expert franchising consultants to ensure that you get excellent advice in establishing the franchise correctly.

> ### ♀ TIP
>
> Ensure that you have a new company to hold the intellectual property (IP) and another separate company from your original trading company to house the head franchisor. This structure will help protect your assets should the unthinkable occur.

According to the ATO, payments received from the franchisee — such as advertising costs, the initial franchise fee, service fees, royalties and training fees — will form part of the franchisor's assessable income for income tax purposes. As these payments are likely to be over $75 000 per annum the franchisor will need to register for GST and charge it accordingly. The franchisor will need to report and remit the GST to the ATO on a quarterly basis. If the franchisee is GST registered, they can claim a GST credit in their business activity statement for the GST paid to the franchisor.

The Franchising Code of Conduct is a mandatory code for all franchise businesses. The Code outlines expected behaviours for both franchisees and franchisors and steps to follow in any dispute resolution process. The Code was updated on 1 April 2025 and includes a new provision that a franchisee must be given a reasonable opportunity to make a return on investment during the term of the agreement.

> ### ⚠ PITFALL
>
> It can be very costly (as much as $350 000) to set up the correct franchising structure as well as complying with all of the requirements of the Franchising Code of Conduct administered through the Australian Competition and Consumer Commission (ACCC).

You also need to maintain a separate set of financial records for each company created in the structure, resulting in higher administration fees such as accounting, tax, audit and Australian Securities and Investments Commission annual registration fees.

88 CROWDFUNDING

As more and more of us spend a large portion of our lives in front of a computer screen and forever looking on social media, the meteoric evolution of crowdfunding as a means to raise funds has been staggering. While there are a number of crowdfunding arrangements which are purely personal or private in nature—such as raising funds for your pet to have surgery—there are tax consequences for other arrangements that have commercial or businesslike activities and have an intention to make a profit.

If you are the promoter in a crowdfunding arrangement, the funds you receive or earn may be assessable income, particularly under a donation-based or a reward-based arrangement, are likely to be assessable income where you:

- use crowdfunding in the course of your employment
- enter into a transaction or scheme with the intention or purpose of making a profit
- receive money or property in the ordinary course of your business.

If you receive money by way of loan it is not assessable but any interest that you repay may be deductible depending on the nature of what the funds were used for. By contrast, the interest income received by the contributor will be assessable income in their return.

If your business receives disaster assistance payments from a crowdfunding platform and uses those funds for business expenses—such as buying feed for livestock—then while the funds are considered assessable income, you are spending it on an allowable deduction so the net tax effect is nil. If those funds are used for personal emergency food and clothing, then the ATO will consider these funds to be non-business related and thus non-assessable.

Funds used to purchase capital assets for your business from crowd-funding are also assessable. But if the purchases are not below the instant asset write-off thresholds (see tip 82), then there may be a timing difference between the income received and the depreciation claim made which may result in an unpopular tax deficit.

If a crowdfunding arrangement is established as an equity-based funding model where the contributors provide money to the promoter in return for an equity interest then the funds will form part of the share capital and will not be assessable in the hands of the promoter. Any future dividends paid to contributors will be assessable to them and any subsequent disposal of shares in the business would have CGT consequences. Any return of capital would generally just reduce the cost base of the initial investment.

⚠ PITFALL

Crowdfunding transactions may also be subject to GST, depending on the type and nature of the arrangement.

⚠ PITFALL

As we saw during the 2019–20 bushfire season, crowdfunding is a great way to appeal to the public to seek funds to help those directly affected by natural disasters. These campaigns usually prove very successful and can raise millions of dollars in the space of a few days. However, a number of these crowdfunding efforts do not produce tax deductions to donors simply if the recipients are not registered with the ATO as a deductible gift recipient.

If you donate money to a disaster victim via a crowdfunding platform but they are not registered as a deductible gift recipient then unfortunately you are not entitled to a tax deduction for your good deed.

👆 TAX FACT

If you donate goods such as groceries, clothes and other items to a deductible gift recipient, you may be able to claim a deduction.

👆 TAX FACT

Large multinational enterprises that operate in Australia are subject to both a 15 per cent global minimum tax and a 15 per cent domestic minimum tax since 1 January 2024.

PART VIII

MISCELLANEOUS

Wouldn't it be great if the tax system fitted nicely into seven parts? Unfortunately, tax legislation is wide and varied. And it will only continue to grow in years to come as the only constant with tax is change.

Part VIII looks at a few more concessions that are available to taxpayers as well as some of the administrative aspects of taxation such as lodgements, penalties, data matching and what to do if you have problems paying your tax debt. I'll also look at earning income overseas and tell you how to get a great accountant.

⚠ PITFALL

While income-protection insurance is deductible, individuals cannot claim a tax deduction for life insurance. Life insurance is only deductible within super.

89 OVERSEAS INCOME

The tax treatment of foreign income by Australian tax residents can be complicated, particularly when foreign tax credits are added into the equation.

☛ TAX FACT

If you are an Australian resident, you are taxed on worldwide income. Any foreign income will need to be included in your tax return as assessable income and you may be entitled to a foreign income tax offset for amounts of foreign tax paid. Non-residents are only taxed on their Australian-sourced income.

The ATO considers you an Australian resident for tax purposes if you meet any of the following conditions:

- you are born and bred in Australia
- you are living permanently in Australia
- you have been living in Australia for at least six months and working the majority of that time at the same job and living at the same place
- you have been living in Australia for more than half of the financial year, except where your usual home is overseas and you do not intend to live in Australia permanently.

⚠ PITFALL

> Pensioners who live or travel overseas for more than six weeks will have their pension paid at the 'outside Australia' rate. After 26 weeks of overseas travel, the pension rate is revised and based on how long you lived in Australia between the age of 16 and the age pension age. Pensioners who have lived in Australia for fewer than 35 years will be paid a reduced pension proportional to their Australian working life residence ratio.

If you are an Australian resident who is engaged in foreign service for a continuous period of 91 days or more you may be eligible for an exemption on Australian tax on this employment income if your employer:

- provides Australian official development assistance
- operates and maintains a public fund for disaster relief for people in a developing country
- is exempt from Australian income tax
- is an Australian Government authority that has deployed you outside Australia as a member of a disciplined force.

⚠ PITFALL

> If you have a foreign currency denominated bank account with a balance greater than A$250 000, you may be subject to Australian tax on any realised foreign currency gains or losses, even if you are merely depositing money and making withdrawals.

If you have been an Australian resident but you leave Australia, then you need to be aware that:

- you are still taxed in Australia on any Australian–sourced income
- any overseas assets are deemed to be disposed for capital gains tax purposes, potentially giving rise to a tax liability
- any HELP or SFSS debts will continue to be indexed.

Which figure do I record in my tax return with respect to foreign currency trading? The balance after losses taken out of profit or only the profit position?

You should be recording the net profit or loss, not just the profit only position. If the losses are greater than the gains then you will probably need to quarantine the losses to future years subject to the non-commercial losses rules.

TAX FACT

The four statutory tests to determine Australian residency for tax purposes are:

- resides test (the primary test)
- domicile test
- 183-day test
- Commonwealth superannuation test

The ATO updated these residency tests for individuals in June 2023 with its Taxation Ruling TR 2023/1 to better reflect modern global work practices and recent court decisions.

90 GETTING A GREAT TAX ACCOUNTANT

A friend once told me that there are two things in life that people need—a good mechanic and a great tax accountant.

TIP

A great tax accountant is just like a surveyor because they know where the boundaries are. They will ensure that you go to the limit with your deductions but that you don't claim so much that you leave yourself open to a visit from the ATO auditors. With their fees being tax-deductible too, why wouldn't you use a professional to handle your affairs?

Taxation is a complex area and deserves the attention of a specialist to give you the right advice to ensure you are maximising deductions yet staying within the regulations.

For some people, tax is a pain and they pay a small fee to get rid of the discomfort. But remember that if you pay peanuts, you get monkeys, so do not base your decision solely on price because a bad accountant could cost you thousands down the track due to a dodgy claim or missing a key strategy to save tax.

✋ TAX FACT

Since 13 November 2023, all businesses with an ABN (including SMSFs but excluding sole traders), must complete an agent nomination process when they engage a new tax agent or seek to provide extra authorisation to your existing agent. The client-to-agent linking is designed to protect against fraud but it is cumbersome and needs to be done via Online services for business with business owners required to install the *myGovID* app. Once nominated, your new agent will have just 28 days to accept the nomination.

⚠ PITFALL

You are not protected if a dodgy accountant claims deductions that you cannot substantiate. If you find an accountant who is dodgy, report them immediately to the authorities. We all hate paying tax, but if everyone pays their fair share then we can expect taxes to be lowered in the future.

The most important thing is to pick an accountant who is a registered tax agent and also a member of a professional body. This at least provides you with some confidence that they are educated and keep reasonably up to date each year with the changing tax laws.

There are four main professionally recognised tax/accountancy bodies in Australia:

- CPA Australia www.cpaaustralia.com.au
- Institute of Chartered Accountants in Australia and New Zealand (CAANZ) www.charteredaccountantsanz.com
- Institute of Public Accountants (IPA) www.publicaccountants.org.au
- The Tax Institute www.taxinstitute.com.au

While it is nice to have an accountant who communicates well, it is more important that they are communicating the right information to you. Ask your friends for recommendations as they can report on their own experience. I also find that a well-constructed website with regular client newsletters and updates that are in plain, simple English is really important. Like mechanics, don't pick someone who treats you like a typical 'dumb' client but rather someone who takes the time to explain things in more depth.

☝ TAX FACT

According to the ATO, the average cost of managing tax affairs claimed by an individual in the 2021–22 financial year was $352. Over 5.84 million taxpayers use a registered tax agent for their tax affairs.

♀ TIP

A great tax accountant, like a top doctor, is likely to be busy so don't get frustrated if they cannot see you at the drop of a hat.

Picking someone who is located near your workplace or business will save you a lot of unnecessary travel time, but you would travel the earth for a great accountant. Also in this day and age of technology, most accountants will be able to deal with you remotely. If you run a business then most accounting software programs that you use (for example, MYOB, QuickBooks or Xero) can be accessed remotely by your accountant.

Finally, trust your instincts. Your finances represent a hugely important matter, so give them the attention they require. If you don't feel comfortable, find another accountant.

♀ TIP

Always ask for a quote in advance of work being prepared by an accountant so you are not shocked when the bill arrives. Unexpected invoices have ended many a client–accountant relationship.

91 LODGING YOUR TAX RETURN

It is compulsory to lodge your income tax return on time. Individuals have to lodge their returns by 31 October each year, unless they are lodging through a registered tax agent. Other entities such as companies, trusts, partnerships and super funds have different lodgement dates that the ATO advises.

> **♀ TIP**
>
> If you are having difficulties getting your tax return lodged by the deadline, or perhaps you have a tax liability, consider appointing a registered tax agent before 31 October. By going on their tax lodgement program you can defer lodging your tax return to 31 March, or even as late as 15 May for some taxpayers.

Registered tax agents get extremely busy around tax deadlines. While some will do anything to help you, including working around the clock, don't leave it to the last minute to see your tax agent as they may be too busy to help.

If you are comfortable with doing your own tax, you can prepare and lodge your tax return online with *myTax*, the ATO's free tax return preparation software program. *myTax* is designed for taxpayers with relatively simple tax affairs. Refunds are generally issued within 12 business days. The software is usually available all year-round, 24 hours per day, seven days per week.

> **♀ TIP**
>
> The *myDeductions* tool within the ATO app is an excellent tool to collect and summarise your deductions throughout the year. It can sync in with your tax return via *myTax* at year end and help make your tax return preparation a lot simpler.

Australian resident taxpayers will be able to use *myTax* if they have income from salary, wages, allowances, bank interest, dividends and/or Australian Government payments. *myTax* has been enhanced to include business and professional items, rental property, partnership and trust distributions as well as capital gains tax, although these calculations can be difficult so make sure you take your time to understand. You can also claim deductions for work-related expenses, expenses related to interest or dividend income, donations and/or the costs of managing their tax affairs, and the only offsets that can be claimed are the senior and pensioner tax offset and/or zone and overseas forces tax offset.

♀TIP

Steps to prepare your income tax return via *myTax*:

1 Check your eligibility to use *myTax* at www.ato.gov.au/MyTax.
2 Wait until the end of August for all information of wages, dividends and interest to filter in from employers, share registries and banks.
3 Log into *myTax* via your myGov account at www.my.gov.au.
4 Review the pre-filled return with information from employers, share registries, banks and private health companies.
5 Enter any missing details — including business and professional items, rental property schedules, distributions from partnerships and trusts, capital gains tax and deductions — to complete your return.
6 Save and print a copy for your records.
7 Lodge online and get an instant confirmation receipt.
8 Receive any refund due within 12 business days.

♀TIP

If your tax affairs are not basic (for example, you run a business or you sold some shares), then consider using a registered tax agent rather than *myTax*.

While *myTax* may be simple to use, ensure you do not rush yourself and miss out on claiming legitimate tax deductions for car, home office or any of the other tips contained in this book!

People who don't send in their tax return by the due date may be charged late-lodgement penalties or may even be prosecuted. Penalties for late lodgement of tax returns can be as high as $1650, as well as good behaviour bonds and jail sentences. The late lodgement of business activity statements (BAS) incurs a fine of $330 for each month late, up to a maximum penalty of $1650 per BAS.

92 AMENDING RETURNS AND OBJECTING TO ASSESSMENTS

Amendments

Whether it is missed interest income or a deduction that you forgot to claim, it is possible to lodge a request with the ATO to amend your income tax return, even long after your original return was lodged and assessed. Generally individuals can request the ATO to amend returns for up to two years after the notice of assessment for the original return is sent to you.

If you have made a mistake or need to amend your tax return, it is important you do so promptly. You can either download the ATO amendment request form or send a letter to the ATO (PO Box 3004, Penrith NSW 2740).

♀ TIP

If you wish to amend your tax return, ensure your amendment request letter contains the following information:

- your name, address and contact phone number
- your TFN
- the income tax year that the amendment relates to
- the reason for the amendment of the return
- the item number of the tax return that requires amendment
- the amount of the amendment
- a declaration that all the information provided, including any attachments, is true and correct and that you have the necessary receipts and other records to support your claim for amendment.

You will also need to sign and date the letter.

⚠ PITFALL

If the amendment of your income tax return results in extra tax required to be paid, the ATO will charge you interest penalties but generally will reduce any other penalties if you have voluntarily told them in advance of any potential audit activity by them of your error.

Objections

If the ATO issues you with a notice of assessment that you disagree with, you don't have to simply 'like it or lump it'. You generally have up to two years to submit an objection to your assessment with the

ATO. If you are objecting to an ATO ruling, other than an assessment, then you generally have only 60 days to lodge your objection to their decision.

All objections must be in writing and signed and dated. You can either download the ATO objection form (NAT 13471) or send a letter to the ATO (PO Box 3524, Albury NSW 2640). The ATO will generally take eight weeks to make a decision about your objection. If you disagree with that decision then you can apply for an independent external review.

Ensure that your objection letter includes the following:

- your name, address and contact phone number
- your TFN
- the income tax year that the amendment relates to
- the reasons why you think that the ATO's original decision is wrong
- the relevant facts, arguments, information and documents that support the reasons you disagree with the ATO decision (including legislation, case law and rulings)
- a declaration that all the information provided, including any attachments, is true and correct
- any supporting documents and information that relate to the decision being reviewed.

🖐 TAX FACT

The ATO issues most individual taxpayers with a tax receipt in conjunction with the original notice of assessment as part of the annual income tax return process.

The tax receipt contains a table showing how your taxes have been allocated to key categories of government expenditure. It also includes information on the level of Australian Government gross debt for the current and previous years.

🎁 BONUS RESOURCES

If you want to lodge an objection you can download and complete the ATO form *Objection form—for taxpayers* (NAT 13471) from the ATO website.

93 ATO DATA MATCHING

Over the past decade, data matching has been a powerful tax compliance tool for the ATO. It has acted as a huge deterrent for taxpayers thinking about not disclosing all of their income.

> ♦ **TAX FACT**
>
> In 2020, the ATO pre-filled over 85 million pieces of data — from the 600 million transactions reported to them — into an estimated 9 million individual tax returns with the use of their data and analytics technology.

When you lodge your income tax return, the onus is firmly on you to make sure that the information contained within the return is complete and correct.

> ♀ **TIP**
>
> Don't try to understate any of your income. If you are on the tax lodgement program of a registered tax agent, then they will generally get a pre-filling report from the ATO to help identify income you may otherwise have missed. It takes time for this information to filter through from the relevant institutions, so the report needs to be seen as a starting point for doing your tax return, not a comprehensive solution.

The ATO has a responsibility to the community to ensure that everyone pays their fair share of tax under the law. If all taxes are correctly collected it means better roads, hospitals and education and perhaps even lower taxes as well. The ATO checks taxpayer compliance with the law by verifying the amounts included in tax returns with information from third parties.

The ATO gets its hands on data from a number of institutions, including the following:

- AUSTRAC, which provides information on banking transactions over $10000
- Australian Electoral Commission
- Australian Securities and Investments Commission (ASIC)
- banks, financial institutions and investment bodies, which provide investment income information such as interest, dividends and managed funds
- businesses in the building and construction industry
- Centrelink
- Child Support Registrar
- credit card and debit card transactions for all merchants with a turnover of less than $10 million
- cryptocurrency designated service providers, which provide purchase and sale information on cryptocurrency transactions
- Department of Immigration and Citizenship
- employers, who provide employment information including PAYG payment summaries
- income protection insurance and landlord insurance
- industry bodies, which provide information for specific transactions
- Medicare Australia, which provides data that enables it to administer the health insurance incentives rebate
- military super
- motor registries, which provide information on individuals and entities that have purchased motor vehicles valued over $10000
- online selling platforms
- passenger movement records from the Department of Home Affairs

- private health insurers, which provide confirmation of health insurance cover and premiums paid
- property management software providers
- real property transactions
- rental bonds
- residential investment property loans
- share economy facilitators
- stock exchanges and share registries, which provide information on share transactions for CGT purposes
- state and territory revenue offices, which provide information on house purchases and disposals
- suppliers, which provide purchase information of purchases greater than a certain amount
- 36 foreign governments that have signed tax information exchange agreements with Australia.

👍 TAX FACT

Over the eight financial years to 2023–24, the ATO used AUSTRAC data to raise liabilities of over $913 million from 20 279 cases alone.

👍 TAX FACT

Businesses in the building and construction industry need to report the total payments they make to each contractor for building and construction services by 28 August each year via a taxable payments annual report (TPAR).

The ATO then matches this data with information lodged in tax returns to detect those who may not be showing all of their income correctly in their tax returns. If there are any discrepancies the ATO will take further action, which may include audits, penalties and, in some cases, imprisonment. Industry-wide data is also analysed (and benchmarking exercises are conducted) to identify trends and to allow the ATO to focus on future compliance risks.

The ATO also identifies people who have never paid taxes or who are behind in lodging tax returns and activity statements, paying taxes or meeting their employer superannuation obligations.

> ### 👆 TAX FACT
>
> The ATO is currently undertaking specific data-matching activities in the following areas:
> - credit and debit cards
> - cryptocurrency
> - insurance
> - investment properties
> - motor vehicle registeries
> - online selling
> - ride-sourcing
> - sharing economy accommodation
> - specialised payment systems.

> ### 💡 TIP
>
> If you suspect that a person or business is being dishonest in their tax affairs or employer obligations, I strongly recommend that you tell the ATO anonymously by completing the online ATO Tip-Off Form: www.ato.gov.au/tipoffform/. The more information that you provide the ATO, the quicker that they can act in stopping the behaviour and recovering unpaid taxes.

94 PROBLEMS PAYING YOUR TAX

You must pay your tax as and when it falls due. But there are times when you simply cannot pay your tax and BAS obligations on time. If you are in this situation contact the ATO immediately to discuss your circumstances. ATO officers are very understanding of your situation and will be as fair and reasonable as possible with you.

> **♀ TIP**
>
> Don't delay the lodgement of your outstanding tax and BAS returns simply because you don't have the money to pay, because there are penalties for late lodgement too.

It is likely that you will need to provide the ATO with your true financial position (such as a list of assets, liabilities, income and expenditure) to show that you are having difficulties meeting your debts as and when they fall due. Depending on your individual circumstances, you may be given an extension of time to pay the ATO.

> **⚠ PITFALL**
>
> If you get an extension of time to pay your taxes, the ATO will impose a general interest charge (GIC), which accrues on your debt until it is paid off in full. The GIC, currently 11.17 per cent, will no longer be tax-deductible from 1 July 2025.

Along with meeting your monthly repayments, you will need to ensure that any future tax returns and activity statements are lodged and paid on time. Failure to do so will be considered a default on your payment arrangement, and will require an explanation to the ATO.

Depending on your individual circumstances, the ATO has the ability to release you from some or all of your tax debts. If paying your tax would cause you 'serious hardship' by preventing you from providing the basic necessities (such as food, shelter, clothing and education) for yourself and your family, then you may apply for this concession.

Taxpayers in this situation will need to complete an 'application for release' form and provide supporting documentation showing how payment of the tax debt will cause serious hardship.

95 ESTATE PLANNING

Death is one of life's few absolute certainties. No matter how rich or poor we may be or become, we are all going to die. Yet despite this absolute certainty, according to the NSW Trustee and Guardian only about 55 per cent of Australians are estimated to have written a will. Even fewer have developed a comprehensive estate plan. If merely from a personal loved ones' perspective, let alone from a tax one, I find these figures absolutely staggering.

Having taught estate planning at university, I could write a whole book on estate planning alone given its complexities and intricacies but given space constraints and your ability to stay awake, I will provide just a few points for you to consider in future discussions with your trusted advisers.

Estate planning has many different meanings but I prefer to think of it as the intergenerational transfer of wealth from one generation to another in a tax effective manner. It involves developing a strategy to deal with your assets after you die with the legal instruments and structures you put in place, such as a will, to transfer your assets to your beneficiaries in the event of death. For those who like having control of their assets, good estate planning could allow you to control these assets from your grave!

> ♀ **TIP**

> If your affairs are complex and you do not have enough knowledge and skills then I strongly recommend seeking assistance from external advisers on more complex estate planning issues such as legal, tax, superannuation and financial planning. A well-planned estate with a valid will and structures such as a testamentary trust will ensure that tax outcomes are achieved and, more importantly, complex family or legal disputes can be prevented.

It is not the only thing but tax is a major consideration in estate planning. A poorly orchestrated estate planning strategy could result in a large portion of your estate going to the ATO which could easily have stayed with your beneficiaries if you structured your affairs slightly better.

Valid will

The very first crucial step in any estate plan is to prepare a valid will. If someone dies without a valid will, this is called 'dying intestate', and their assets are distributed according to the inheritance laws of the states and territories of Australia. In this case there is a risk that the undocumented intentions of the deceased person in relation to their estate may not be fully acted on.

◆ TAX FACT

The key requirements for a valid will include:

- it must be in writing
- it must be signed by the will maker (also known as the testator) who must be at least age 18
- the will maker must have the testamentary capacity to make the will and understand its nature and effect at the time of signing
- the will maker must sign the will in front of two adult witnesses who are independent.

♀ TIP

Making a valid will is not a once in a lifetime, set and forget process. Assets come and go and beneficiaries' circumstances (such as their tax, health and marital status) do change. Have a process in place to periodically review your estate planning strategy in conjunction with your advisers, including your legal, tax, superannuation and financial advisers.

Capital gains tax

Depending on the marginal tax rates of different beneficiaries, intestacy could potentially lead to an overall inequality in the distribution of an estate due to higher rates of tax payable by some beneficiaries. An example of this might be the otherwise good natured decision to leave one half of an estate which was in cash to one beneficiary on a low income (essentially tax free) and the other half which was in a share portfolio with substantial unrealised capital gains tax to another beneficiary on the highest marginal tax rate. Good estate planning can avoid this result. When preparing a will, the will maker and their advisers can assess opportunities to manage the tax implications for beneficiaries.

While death can be sudden, it may be possible to do some planning before you die:

- Use any capital losses that are accumulated or unrealised prior to death, as these cannot be passed on to beneficiaries.
- Bequeath share portfolios to beneficiaries on lower taxable incomes so that tax paid on income and capital gains in the future are minimal and the capital is preserved for as long as possible.
- If the estate is substantial and there are children under age 18 who are potential beneficiaries, consider establishing a testamentary trust so they can access the favourable adult marginal tax rates.

> **♀ TIP**
>
> As discussed in tip 47 capital gains tax can have special CGT rules apply to the transfer of any shares from a deceased estate. You should seek specialist advice in relation to the CGT implications of passing on or disposing of the assets of a deceased estate. Where possible, keep complete records of your CGT assets as these will be needed by your executor and any beneficiary who receives a CGT asset from the estate.

Testamentary trusts

A testamentary trust is a trust created via a clause in the 'testament' (or valid will) of an individual but does not get established until after the individual dies. It functions in a similar way to a discretionary family trust, with certain provisions of the will operating like a trust deed. A testamentary trust is an indirect way of managing your family's wealth after your death. Probably its biggest benefit is that there are substantial tax advantages relating to testamentary trusts, including distributions to minors being taxed at the more favourable adult rates. While you obviously will not be around to oversee the management of the trust itself, you will have some comfort knowing that your loved ones will be looked after financially and not savaged by the ATO.

The cost of administering a testamentary trust can easily negate any potential benefits and intended tax outcomes as it needs to lodge a tax return for every financial year that it is in existence as well as maintain proper trust account records such as trustee resolutions and detailed financial statements. There may also be some substantial tax planning required each year to properly understand the tax profile of potential beneficiaries to minimise any taxes payable.

Superannuation and binding death nominations

With superannuation now playing such a large part in a person's net wealth it is vitally important that you understand the legal and tax issues around estate planning and superannuation. Most importantly, superannuation is not an estate asset; on death it does not automatically flow to the estate of the deceased.

In the absence of a binding death benefit nomination, the trustee of your superannuation fund will generally pay a death benefit in accordance with the governing rules of the fund and relevant law. He or she will have the discretion to pay your superannuation benefits to any of your superannuation dependents instead of your estate. This discretion effectively overrides your wishes in your will, which only deals with the estate assets and deferring tax consequences. Where a nomination is in place, the benefits will be paid to the nominated beneficiaries. A binding death benefit nomination is a way to override this trustee discretion.

To make a valid binding death benefit nomination it must:
- be made to the trustee of your superannuation fund in writing and clearly set out the proportion of the benefit to be paid to each person nominated.
- be signed by the member in the presence of two witnesses over 18 years of age and who are not nominated as beneficiaries

- contain a signed witness declaration
- be sent to (and received by) the trustee of your superannuation fund
- be no more than three years old.

Once you have made the nomination, it will be valid for three years from the date it was signed, or non-lapsing depending on the superannuation trust deed options. You can renew, change, update or revoke a nomination at any time. This is important because the tax-free status of a child beneficiary can change in an instant when they go from a minor to an adult.

⚠ PITFALL

As discussed in tip 70, it is crucial to strongly consider tax implications when nominating your beneficiaries of your superannuation benefits. Whilst lump-sum payments to dependants (your spouse or minor children) are tax-free, lump-sum payments to non-dependants (adult children) are taxed at 17 per cent on the taxed element while the untaxed element is taxed at a maximum rate of 32 per cent. A simple mistake like this could send tens of thousands of dollars straight to the taxman.

Administering a deceased estate

If you become an executor of a deceased estate, you need to understand your tax obligations that were outlined in tip 11, including:

- notifying the ATO that you have been appointed as executor
- lodging a final date of death return plus any outstanding prior year returns for the deceased
- lodging any subsequent trust tax returns for the deceased estate including the payment of any resulting tax on its income
- providing beneficiaries with the information they need to include distributions in their own returns and, in certain cases, paying tax on their behalf.

96 PRIVATE ANCILLARY FUNDS

If running your own SMSF was the big money fad in the first decade of this century, then having your own family's charitable foundation—or ancillary fund—seems to be the latest must-have financial accessory for wealthy Australians today.

Ancillary funds are charitable trusts for the purpose of making grants to deductible gift recipients (DGRs) for public benefit in Australia. There are two types of ancillary funds, private and public. Private ancillary funds (PAFs) are established and funded by an individual, a family or a small group of donors and may not accept donations from the general public.

✋ TAX FACT

According to the ATO, in 2022 there were 2097 private and 1450 public ancillary funds in Australia with combined net assets of $14.16 billion. They received $2.50 billion in donations in that year and distributed $1.27 billion in grants.

Similar to SMSFs, private ancillary funds are tax-advantageous vehicles established by trust deed, who cannot operate a business nor pay its founders/trustees yet have a number of reporting obligations (including preparing audited financial statements and lodging tax returns) and are required to distribute a minimum amount each year. The sceptical side of me thinks that accountants and/or financial planners are the ones who have driven the rapid growth for both industries just so they can create more work for themselves!

PAFs will require a corporate trustee and can apply to become a DGR themselves so that it can receive donations that are tax-deductible to the donor. Each trustee must agree to comply with the *Taxation Administration (Private Ancillary Fund) Guidelines 2019* and also issue receipts for any tax-deductible gifts.

If you made a sizeable windfall gain during the year then consider establishing your own private ancillary fund and make a tax-deductible donation to reduce any potential tax bill.

During each financial year, apart from the year the fund is established, a private ancillary fund must distribute at least 5 per cent of the market value of the fund's net assets as at the start of the financial year.

👍 TAX FACT

A PAF must distribute at least $11000 to DGRs during a financial year if both of the following applies:

- the calculation of the 5 per cent minimum annual distribution is less than $11000
- any of the expenses of the fund in relation to that financial year are paid directly or indirectly from the fund's assets or income.
- If the fund is worth less than $11000 then it must distribute the remaining funds.

As a DGR, PAFs must keep adequate accounting and other records that detail and explain all transactions that are relevant to its status as a DGR. The current penalty for not keeping proper records for at least five years after the completion of the transactions is $3300.

⚠ PITFALL

Penalties may apply if a PAF does not meet the minimum annual distribution requirements, but it can apply to the ATO to reduce the minimum annual distribution rate (NAT 74894).

Trustees are required to lodge an ancillary fund return in conjunction with an annual information statement with the Australian Charities and Not-for-profits Commission (ACNC) each financial year.

Since 1 July 2024, all not-for-profit organisations with an active ABN need to lodge a NFP self-review return to maintain its income tax exemption. The NFP self-review return requires the NFP's to consider their purpose and activities against specific requirements and needs to be submitted by 31 October through either Online services for business, or a registered tax agent using Online services for agents. More information is available at www.ato.gov.au/NFPtaxexempt.

As a way of encouraging wealthy individuals to increase distributions (beyond 5 per cent) to DGRs that were struggling as a result of the COVID-19 pandemic, the government amended the minimum annual distribution rules for PAFs.

Private ancillary funds that exceed their minimum annual distribution rate for the 2019–20 and 2020–21 financial years, by a total of five per cent or more, will have a lower minimum annual distribution rate of 4 per cent in future years. The credit balance will reduce by 2 per cent for each year that the PAF only distributes the reduced 4 per cent minimum until such time that the credit is reduced to less than 2 percent at which point in must return back to the normal 5 per cent minimum.

✏️ **EXAMPLE**

The Tax Family Foundation is a private ancillary fund that increased its annual distribution — beyond the minimum 5 per cent required — to help several DGRs survive during the COVID-19 pandemic.

The Tax Family Foundation made an annual distribution of 11 per cent in 2019–20 and 8 per cent in 2020–21 being a cumulative 19 per cent over the two financial years. After reducing the amount by 10 per cent (being the minimum 5 per cent annual distribution requirement over two years), it has a credit amount of 9 per cent and thus eligible for a reduced minimum annual distribution rate for at least four years.

If the Tax Family Foundation only distributes the 4 per cent minimum in each of the 2021–22, 2022–23, 2023–24 and 2024–25 financial years then from the 2025–26 financial year its minimum annual distribution rate will return to 5 per cent.

TABLE 8.1: example of the reduced minimum annual distribution rate for PAFs

	2019–20	2020–21	2021–22	2022–23	2023–24	2024–25
Annual distribution	11%	8%	4%	4%	4%	4%
Credit available	–	9%	9%	7%	5%	3%
Less: credit reduction	–	–	–2%	–2%	–2%	–2%
Credit remaining	–	9%	7%	5%	3%	1%

> **♀TIP**
>
> Before you make a donation to charity, check that they have deductible gift recipient (DGR) status, otherwise you will not be able to claim the deduction in your return.

97 LEVIES

Medicare levy surcharge

For the past 40 years, the Medicare scheme has provided Australians with greater access to health care. It has been funded by a Medicare levy paid by individual taxpayers who are also Australian residents. The levy is charged by the ATO based on 2 per cent of your taxable income via your notice of assessment each year.

> **🖐 TAX FACT**
>
> The Medicare levy was raised on 1 July 2014 by half a percentage point to 2 per cent to provide a funding stream for the National Disability Insurance Scheme (NDIS).

If you or your dependants do not have private health insurance and your 'adjusted taxable income' was above a certain amount, you may have to pay an additional Medicare levy surcharge on top of the standard 2 per cent levy.

⚠ PITFALL

If you are over 30 and don't have private health cover there are lifetime health cover penalties that apply when you subsequently take out cover. For each year over age 30 that you delay in getting basic hospital cover, you will have to pay an extra 2 per cent on your premium, up to a maximum of 70 per cent, when you finally take out the cover.

The Medicare levy surcharge is an additional levy of up to 1.5 per cent, charged on your adjusted taxable income, which is the sum of:

- your taxable income
- your reportable super contributions
- your net investment losses
- your total reportable fringe benefits
- any amount on which family trust distribution tax has been paid.

♀ TIP

The size of your Medicare levy surcharge is affected by your level of income, your marital status, the number of children you have and your age, as outlined in tables 8.2 and 8.3 (overleaf). If you earn more than the adjusted taxable income threshold, take out basic hospital cover to avoid the Medicare levy surcharge, as it will probably be cheaper.

If you and your dependants have private health insurance, you may be eligible for a refundable tax rebate. It can be received as a refund even if you do not have to pay any tax. Similar to the Medicare levy surcharge, this private health rebate is affected by your income, marital status and age.

TABLE 8.2: medicare levy surcharge and private health insurance rebate (singles) (2025–26)

Adjusted taxable income	Medicare levy surcharge	Rebate if under age 65	Rebate if aged 65–69 years	Rebate if over age 70
Up to $101000	Nil	24.288%	28.337%	32.385%
$101001–$118000	1%	16.192%	20.240%	24.288%
$118001–$158000	1.25%	8.095%	12.143%	16.192%
over $158000	1.5%	0%	0%	0%

Source: © Australian Taxation Office for the Commonwealth of Australia.

TABLE 8.3: medicare levy surcharge and private health insurance rebate (couples or single parents) (2025–26)

Adjusted taxable income (total)*	Medicare levy surcharge	Rebate if under age 65	Rebate if aged 65–69 years	Rebate if over age 70
Up to $202000	Nil	24.288%	28.337%	32.385%
$202001–$236000	1%	16.192%	20.240%	24.288%
$236001–$316000	1.25%	8.095%	12.143%	16.192%
over $316000	1.5%	0%	0%	0%

*The threshold rises by $1500 for each dependent child born after the first.
Source: © Australian Taxation Office for the Commonwealth of Australia.

♀TIP

If you know that you are going to fall above a higher income threshold (or you are unsure what your income level will be), then contact your private health provider at the start of the year and reduce the rebate that you receive upfront. Otherwise you might get a nasty surprise when you get your tax assessment and find out that you have to pay back a part or all of your rebate that you were not entitled to receive.

Those with incomes just below each threshold a word of warning that you move above a higher income threshold if your income increases (known as 'bracket creep'). For those with private health insurance, your rebate percentage entitlement may decrease. For those who do not have the appropriate level of private patient hospital cover, you may have to pay either the Medicare levy surcharge or if you paid the surcharge in the previous year, the rate of the surcharge may increase.

Consider prepaying up to 12 months of private medical cover before the end of the current tax year if you think your taxable income in the subsequent financial year will take you above one of the private health insurance rebate 'income thresholds' in table 8.1 (singles) and table 8.2 (couples). The situation might arise if you are planning on realising a large capital gain or perhaps receiving a big bonus after 30 June. By implementing this strategy you will be able to get the higher rebate percentage back to you in the current year.

98 ZONE AND OVERSEAS FORCES TAX OFFSETS

If you lived or worked in a remote area or served in forces overseas during the financial year you may be able to claim a tax offset.

Zone tax offset

This is often a forgotten claim—particularly if you use an accountant outside of the region where you live. The offset is available if you lived in a remote or isolated part of Australia, not including an offshore oil or gas rig, for at least half of the financial year.

The ATO classifies remote areas into two zones—zone A and zone B—and designates special areas within these zones. If you are unsure whether you are in a remote area, the ATO has an Australian zone list available on its website.

To qualify for the zone tax offset, you must have worked or lived in a remote area for 183 days or more during the current financial year or, if you haven't previously claimed the zone tax offset, 183 days or more in total during the current and previous financial years—but less than 183 days in the current year and less than 183 days in the previous financial year.

Note that the time spent in a remote area does not have to be continuous.

'Fly-in fly-out' and 'drive-in drive-out' workers are not eligible for the zone tax offset when their normal residence is not within a zone.

Some tax agents who live in capital cities do not automatically think of this tax offset, so it is wise to prompt them if you do live in a zone area.

Overseas forces tax offset

If you have served during the financial year in a specified overseas locality as a member of either the Australian defence forces or the United Nations forces, and your income relating to that service was not specifically exempt from tax, you may be eligible for an overseas forces tax offset.

You can only claim for either the overseas forces tax offset or the zone tax offset in your income tax return, even if you qualify for both. So pick the one that gives the higher claim.

To claim the full overseas forces tax offset, you must have served in one or more overseas localities for 183 days or more during the financial year. A portion of the offset may still be claimed even if your overseas service was fewer than 183 days.

The tax offset amounts are shown in table 8.4.

TABLE 8.4: zone and overseas forces tax offsets (2024–25)

Your circumstances	Zone A	Zone B	Special area	Overseas forces
You were single with no dependent child or student for whole of year	$338	$57	$1173	$338
You are able to claim the maximum dependant (invalid and carer) tax offset $3300)	$1988	$717	$2823	$1988

Source: © Australian Taxation Office for the Commonwealth of Australia.

99 TAX-EFFECTIVE INVESTMENTS

Around May and June each year, there are a number of accountants and financial planners who try to promote tax-effective investments in agribusiness and forestry products.

> **♀ TIP**
>
> A good financial adviser will recommend that you have no more than 5 per cent of your investment portfolio in tax-effective investments, given the high risk associated with them.

The ATO has labelled these investments as 'aggressive tax planning' products and for good reason—these investments have copped a lot of bad press in recent years thanks to some projects going into administration, resulting in their investors losing potentially thousands of dollars.

👍 TAX FACT

Investments in agribusiness or forestry products generally have 100 per cent tax-deductibility in the first year. Different from investments in shares or properties, if you invest say $100 000 in these types of investments you may get a tax deduction of $100 000.

💡 TIP

Before you sign up to any tax-effective scheme, ensure that there is a product ruling for the project issued by the ATO so that you can get some certainty on the tax benefits contained within the product disclosure statement.

Used the right way, they can be a very good tax-planning strategy; for example, they can help level out the tax on any capital gains or bonus during a financial year.

But sometimes these investments sound too good to be true. Potential investors must form their own view about the commercial and financial viability of the product. Take care before you invest because while you are getting a tax deduction you are still risking the amount not covered by your marginal tax rate. If the project doesn't generate its projected returns, you will be out of pocket after tax.

⚠ PITFALL

A product ruling issued by the ATO in no way guarantees the actual project, or whether it is even commercially viable. The ATO does not verify that the projected returns will be achieved or are reasonably based.

If the project is ultimately not carried out as described to the ATO originally, investors may also lose the protection of the tax benefits outlined in the product ruling.

100 TAX PLANNING AS A 365-DAY PROCESS

It always surprises me when people think that tax planning only occurs in June each year. Well, it may for those who are not very organised. But if you want to save as much as legitimately possible on your largest expense, I encourage you to start tax planning on the first day of July each year.

Throughout this book there are tips that are probably more applicable for action at the start of the year than at the end of the year.

> **♀ TIP**
>
> Tax planning should be a 365-day per year exercise, not one merely carried out in the last few weeks before 30 June. A lot of these strategies are just as useful on 1 July as they are on 30 June.
>
> For example, a strategy such as super co-contribution is a lot more manageable if you take out $20 per week over a year, rather than trying to find $1000 at the end of the year.

For wealthier people, there is an opportunity at the start of each year to have a regular amount of each month's salary sacrificed into superannuation so that you take advantage of the concessionally taxed contribution limits.

Negative gearing and depreciation have much more impact when spread over a whole year rather than just a few days. A logbook is the best way of maximising your car deductions for work-related purposes but you can't just do one on 30 June—it takes 12 weeks of diligence in keeping accurate records.

> **⚠ PITFALL**
>
> Tax agents cannot wave a magic wand if you don't do the basics and keep your receipts throughout the year for your work- or business-related expenses. The ATO's rule in most circumstances is that no receipt results in no deduction.

101 JUST DO IT!

Over the past few hundred pages you have read some great strategies to save money on your taxes — legally. Now it is time to take action.

> **♀ TIP**
>
> I am a big fan of the famous Nike advertising campaign. When you get great advice then 'Just Do It'. I get really annoyed when my clients don't follow through because they forgot or were too lazy to get around to it.

Thank you for taking the time to read this book. I hope it has been of benefit to you. Over time, I have no doubt that these strategies will save you significant amounts of money — and during tough times, every single dollar counts!

> **👆 TAX FACT**
>
> As mentioned in the introduction, not every single tip outlined in this book is applicable to everyone. But I guarantee you that at least one of these tips will save you more than the cost of this book. In fact, the purchase of this book as reference material for your tax affairs will be tax-deductible. Do you still have that receipt?

You will be surprised how many slackos there are that miss out on easy money despite how simple some of these strategies are. Take the superannuation co-contribution, for example.

If you procrastinated every year since the introduction of super co-contribution in 2003 (and there are a lot of people out there who have) and kept on forgetting to contribute post-tax dollars into super, you have missed out on potentially $18 500 of free money from the government. With savings generally doubling every ten years, your retirement savings could be almost $37 000 higher as well.

> **♀ TIP**
>
> The simplest way to remind yourself to action something is to put a follow-up reminder in your calendar. If you have a computer with an online calendar, such as the one in Microsoft Outlook, you can set up reminders on a regular basis as 'new appointments'. When the reminder pops up on your screen in the future, don't 'dismiss' until you have actioned it. Press 'snooze' instead.

> **⚠ PITFALL**
>
> Research has found that 100 per cent of action plans that are not started result in the goals set out in the action plans not being achieved.

Can you and your family afford to miss out on this amount of money simply by leaving things to next week or next year?

I wish you and your family much happiness and hope that life is not too taxing!

GLOSSARY

$1000 upfront tax concession: If you acquire ESS interests under a taxed-upfront scheme that meets certain conditions, you will be eligible to receive a tax concession of up to $1000 if your taxable income after adjustments is $180 000 or less.

30-day rule: If you dispose of your ESS interest within 30 days after the deferred taxing point, the deferred taxing point becomes the date of that disposal.

45-day rule: See *holding period rule*.

ABN: Australian Business Number; a unique identifying number issued to all entities registered in the Australian Business Register.

ABR: Australian Business Register; the extensive database of identity information provided by businesses when they register for an ABN www.abr.gov.au.

ACCC: Australian Competition and Consumer Commission; government organisation responsible for ensuring compliance with the *Trade Practices Act 1974* www.accc.gov.au.

accruals basis: If you account for an invoice but do not receive the cash, you are using an accruals basis of accounting; you can use the cash basis if your annual turnover is $1 million or less.

adjusted taxable income: The sum of:

- taxable income
- reportable fringe benefits
- reportable superannuation contributions
- total net investment loss.

allowable deduction: An expense you can deduct from your assessable income.

APRA: Australian Prudential Regulation Authority—APRA is responsible for regulating certain types of super funds www.apra.gov.au.

ASIC: Australian Securities & Investments Commission—the corporate, markets and financial services regulator in Australia www.asic.gov.au.

assessable income: The income you derive, before deducting allowable deductions, that is liable to tax.

associate: Associates include people and entities closely associated with you, such as relatives, or closely connected companies or trustees of a trust (other than the trustee of an employee share trust). For example, a partner in a partnership is an associate of the partnership and an individual's spouse is an associate of the individual. You may also be an associate of a self managed super fund in which you are a member or a family trust of which you are a beneficiary.

ASX: Australian Securities Exchange — the marketplace for trading shares, bonds and other securities in Australia www.asx.com.au.

ATO: Australian Taxation Office — the ATO's role is to manage and collect tax as well as act as regulator of self managed super funds in Australia www.ato.gov.au.

AUSTRAC: Australian Transaction Reports and Analysis Centre — Australia's anti-money laundering and counter-terrorism financing regulator and specialist financial intelligence unit www.austrac.gov.au.

Australian Apprenticeship Support Loan: A loan paid in instalments totalling up to $25 374 over four years to assist eligible apprentices with everyday costs while they complete their apprenticeship www.australianapprenticeships.gov.au.

BAS: Business activity statement — a statement under the pay-as-you-go system that you prepare at the end of each quarter to remit GST, PAYG withholding and PAYG instalments.

beneficiary: A person who is potentially entitled to a payment from a trust.

bitcoin: The first and most popular decentralised cryptocurrency and worldwide payment system which works without a central bank or single administrator.

blockchain: A continuously growing list of records, called blocks, which are linked and secured using cryptography, the public transaction ledger for the cryptocurrency bitcoin.

bonus shares: Free shares issued by a company usually in proportion to your current share holdings.

brokerage fee: The fee charged by a stockbroker when you buy or sell shares.

business real property: A property that is used wholly or exclusively by one or more businesses.

buy contract note: An invoice you receive from a stockbroker at the time you buy shares. It will summarise the details of the transaction and can be used to calculate a capital gain or capital loss for taxation purposes.

CAANZ: Institute of Chartered Accountants in Australia and New Zealand—one of the four main professionally recognised tax/accounting bodies in Australia (along with CPA Australia, the IPA and the Tax Institute) www.charteredaccountantsanz.com.

call option: The right, but not the obligation, to buy the underlying shares at an agreed price on or before the date of expiration.

capital expenditure: Money spent on assets such as plant and equipment, goodwill, buildings, patents and copyrights.

capital loss: The loss you incur when you sell CGT assets such as shares for a price that's below their reduced cost base; under Australian tax law a capital loss can only be offset against a capital gain.

capital protection loan: A loan to buy shares where you can protect yourself from incurring a loss if your share portfolio falls in value.

cash basis: If you issue (or receive) an invoice but do not account for the sale (or purchase) until the cash is received (or paid), you are using a cash basis of accounting; you can use the cash basis if your annual turnover is $1 million or less.

CCS: Child care subsidy—government benefit that helps eligible families with the cost of child care.

cents per kilometre method: One of the two methods of claiming a deduction for car expenses. You can use this method up to a maximum of 5000 business kilometres at a flat rate of 88 cents per kilometre.

CGT: Capital gains tax—the tax payable on the disposal of an investment asset that was acquired after 19 September 1985. It is not a separate tax, just part of your income tax. The most common way you make a capital gain (or capital loss) is by selling or disposing of assets such as real estate, shares or managed fund investments.

CGT asset register: A register you keep to record all CGT assets you own, such as your share portfolio.

CGT event: Normally arises when there's a change in ownership of a CGT asset.

company: A separate legal entity, registered by ASIC, that can carry on a business in its own name; a company raises capital through the issue of shares.

company tax rate: 25 per cent of a small company's taxable income (30 per cent for companies with aggregated annual turnover greater than $50 million).

complying super fund: A super fund that is regulated by the ATO and has been issued with a notice of compliance; complying funds that meet the *SIS Act 1993* standards qualify for a concessional tax rate.

concessional tax rate: Super funds that comply with the *SIS Act 1993* qualify for the concessional tax rate of 15 per cent; non-complying super funds do not receive the concessional tax rate and are taxed at 45 per cent. Contributions made by individuals earning more than $250000 are taxed at 30 per cent.

condition of release: A condition, normally retirement, that must be satisfied before you can access your benefits in a superannuation fund.

contribution: The money or asset directly contributed by an individual, an employer or another party into a super fund.

cost base: The cost base of an asset is generally what it costs you. It is made up of five elements:

- the money you paid or property you gave for the asset
- the incidental costs of acquiring or selling it (for example, brokerage and stamp duty)
- the costs of owning it (generally this will not apply to shares because you will usually have claimed or be entitled to claim these costs as tax deductions)
- the costs associated with increasing or preserving its value, or with installing or moving it
- the cost to you to preserve or defend your title or rights to it.

COVID-19: coronavirus disease of 2019 — the pandemic virus that created both a global health and economic crises in 2020–22 which led to a number of government relief measures. The illness affects the lungs and airways and has led to millions of deaths amongst the three quarters of a billion infected cases worldwide.

CPA Australia: One of the four main professionally recognised tax/accounting bodies in Australia (along with CAANZ, the IPA and the Tax Institute) www.cpaaustralia.com.au.

CPI: Consumer price index—the general inflation index prepared by the Australian Bureau of Statistics that measures the change in the price of a fixed basket of goods bought by households.

crowdfunding: the practice of raising money from a large number of people via an online fundraising platform to fund a project or venture.

cryptocurrency: A digital asset designed to work as a medium of exchange that uses cryptography to secure its transactions, to control the creation of additional units, and to verify the transfer of assets. Uses decentralised control through a blockchain, which is a public transaction database, functioning as a distributed ledger.

crystallise: To dispose of shares in order to create or realise a capital gain or capital loss.

deferred taxing point: The earliest of the following times:

- seven years after you acquired a share/right between 1 July 2009 and 30 June 2015
- 15 years after you acquired a share/right from 1 July 2015
- the time you cease the employment in respect of which you acquired the share/right
- the time when there is no real risk of forfeiture and the scheme no longer genuinely restricts the disposal of the share/right.

DeFi: Decentralised finance. It is an Ethereum blockchain-based form of finance that is conducted without relying on a financial intermediary.

dependants: People you look after who need your financial support; usually spouse and minor children.

depreciation: A non-cash expense which is the decline in value of an asset over time.

derived: Income you earn that is liable for tax.

DGR: Deductible gift recipient.

DICTO: Dependant (invalid and carer) tax offset— available to taxpayers who maintain a dependant who is genuinely unable to work due to carer obligation or disability. In this instance, eight dependency tax offsets have been consolidated into a single, streamlined and non-refundable offset.

DIDO: Drive-in drive-out—an arrangement where the employee drives a considerable distance from/to their normal residence to work for a number of days on a regular and rotational basis, and has a number of days off that are not the same days in consecutive weeks. Special LAFHA rules apply.

directors: Appointed by shareholders to manage and run the day-to-day operations of a company.

discounted capital gain: A 50 per cent reduction on the capital gain on disposal of CGT assets that were owned for at least 12 months.

discretionary trust: A trust where the trustee has discretion as to how the trust net income should be distributed to the beneficiaries.

dividend: A distribution of profit paid to shareholders of a company in proportion to the number of shares owned.

dividend reinvestment plan: A scheme where a company gives shareholders the option of reinvesting dividends in the form of new shares in the company, rather than receiving the dividends in cash.

Division 7A: A section of the Tax Act that contains anti-avoidance provisions which are aimed at preventing private company owners and their associates from avoiding dividend taxation by trying to access company profits in another form besides dividends.

Division 293 tax: A section of the Tax Act which reduces the tax concession on super contributions for individuals with income greater than the Division 293 threshold of $250 000 by increasing the superannuation tax rate from 15 to 30 per cent.

DIY super: Do-it-yourself superannuation, also known as an SMSF.

downsizer contributions: Contributions made by those aged 55 and over into superannuation within 90 days of sale of their home (of at least ten years) up to a maximum of $300 000 each. Excluded from the non-concessional contribution limit.

DRP: Dividend reinvestment plan.

election: When a taxpayer makes a choice, usually in writing, with respect to adopting a certain tax law ahead of another.

ESIC: Early stage innovation company. An unlisted Australian company with turnover less than $200 000 and expenses under $1 million in the preceding year plus satisfy one of two innovations tests. Special tax incentives are available to its sophisticated investors.

ESS: Employee share scheme; a scheme under which shares, stapled securities and rights (including options) to acquire shares and stapled securities in a company are provided to its employees (including current, past or prospective employees and their associates) in relation to their employment.

ESS interests: Shares, stapled securities, or rights (including options) to acquire shares or stapled securities.

ESS statement: An annual statement that shows an estimate of any discounts you or your associates have received on your ESS interests.

estate planning: The intergenerational transfer of wealth from one generation to another in a tax effective manner to effectively control your assets from the grave.

ether: A popular cryptocurrency whose blockchain is generated by the Ethereum platform.

ETP: Employment termination payment (previously known as an eligible termination payment); a lump-sum payment made due to your employment being terminated.

Export Market Development Grant: A scheme that provides grants to small and medium-sized businesses who incur eligible export promotion expenses. Administered by Austrade.

family discretionary trust: A trust whose membership is ordinarily made up of family beneficiaries; the trustee has discretion to distribute trust net income to certain beneficiaries.

FBT: Fringe benefits tax.

FIFO: Fly-in fly-out—an arrangement where the employee flies from/to their normal residence to work for a number of days on a regular and rotational basis and has a number of days off that are not the same days in consecutive weeks. Special LAFHA rules apply.

financial year: The period from 1 July to 30 June the following year.

foreign tax credit: Foreign tax paid on income derived from overseas sources that can be offset against Australian tax payable on taxable income derived from worldwide sources.

franked dividends: Dividends paid by an Australian resident company from profits that have had Australian company tax paid on them.

franking credits: The amounts of tax paid previously by a company that are allocated to dividends paid to shareholders; the taxpayer receives the credits in their income tax assessment to avoid double taxation; also known as imputation credits.

GIC: General interest charge—interest rate imposed by the ATO for late payment of tax. Not deductible from 1 July 2025.

GST: Goods and services tax—10 per cent tax on goods and services.

HELP: Higher Education Loan Program.

holding period rule: The rule where shareholders must continuously hold shares 'at risk' for at least 45 days (90 days for preference shares) around the ex-dividend date in order to be eligible for the franking tax offset. However, under the small shareholder exemption, this rule does not apply if your total franking credit entitlement is below $5000, which is roughly equivalent to receiving a fully franked dividend of $11 666 (based on the current tax rate of 30 per cent for companies).

IAS: Instalment activity statement—a statement under the pay-as-you-go system that you prepare at the end of each reporting period disclosing certain income that is liable to tax.

imputation credit: See *franking credits*.

income tax: A federal tax that you pay on taxable income you derive.

income tax return: An annual form lodged with the ATO disclosing your taxable income.

incurred: The point in time when you can legally claim a deduction, usually when you have a commitment and a legal obligation to make a payment for certain goods and services you receive.

indeterminate right: A right to acquire at a future time either:

- shares or cash (at the discretion of your employer)
- a number of shares, where that number cannot be determined at the time of acquisition of the right but will be determined at a later time.

initial repairs: Costs to rectify damage, defects or deterioration that existed at the time of purchasing a property and considered to be capital in nature and not deductible for tax purposes.

instalment warrant: A form of derivative or financial product that entails borrowing to invest in an underlying asset, such as a share or real property, with limited risk to the investor. The underlying asset is held in trust during the life of the loan to provide limited security for the lender. The investor is required to pay one or more future instalments to the lender.

investment strategy: A document setting out how you intend to invest your benefits in an SMSF; it must be in writing and must consider investment risks, the likely returns and whether you have sufficient cash on hand to discharge liabilities when they fall due.

IP: Intellectual property.

IPA: IPA Institute of Public Accountants, formerly National Institute of Accountants—one of the four main professionally recognised tax/accounting bodies in Australia (along with CAANZ, CPA Australia and the Tax Institute) www.publicaccountants.org.au.

ITAA 1936: *The Income Tax Assessment Act 1936.*

ITAA 1997: *The Income Tax Assessment Act 1997.*

JobSeeker: Income support for those who are unemployed, looking for work and aged between 22 and the Age Pension age, or are sick or injured and cannot perform usual work duties.

joint tenants: A legal arrangement in which two or more people own a property together, each with equal rights and obligations. When one of the owners in a joint tenancy dies, that owner's interest in the property passes direct to the survivors without the property having to go through the courts.

LAFHA: Living-away-from-home allowance—a tax-free allowance paid to employees who are required to perform their work duties away from their usual place of residence.

litecoin: A cryptocurrency that uses Scrypt as a hashing algorithm.

LITO: Low-income tax offset.

LMR: Lost members register—a register maintained by the ATO showing a list of lost and unclaimed super.

low-income tax offset: A general tax offset you can claim if your taxable income is below a certain threshold; the tax offset is reduced by 1.5 cents for every dollar you earn above the threshold. Taxpayers who receive this offset are also entitled to the low to middle income tax offset.

low-value pool: A pool of depreciable assets, each with a written-down value under $1000, which can be depreciated at a more favourable pool rate of 37.5 per cent per annum.

margin call: The shortfall required if the value of your shares, funded by a margin loan, falls below a certain level.

margin loan: A form of borrowing to fund a share portfolio.

marginal tax rate: The rate of tax applicable to the last dollar of your taxable income; your average tax rate on your entire taxable income is generally lower than your marginal tax rate.

Medicare levy: A 2 per cent levy charged on your taxable income.

Medicare levy surcharge: An extra levy (up to 1.5 per cent) charged on taxable income when taxpayers do not have private health insurance and their 'adjusted taxable income' is above a certain amount.

***myDeductions*:** The tool within the ATO app that you can download onto a mobile device to make it easier and more convenient to keep your tax deductions and income records all in one place. Syncs in with *myTax* at financial year end.

***myTax*:** The ATO's online tax preparation program for self-preparers with simple tax affairs www.ato.gov.au/MyTax.

NDIS: National Disability Insurance Scheme - Tax-exempt assistance received by eligible people with a disability www.ndis.gov.au

negative gearing: Occurs when the net rental income from an investment property, after deducting other expenses, is less than the interest on the borrowings, a very popular tax strategy employed by Australians; these properties are purchased with the assistance of borrowed funds and partly repaid by the tax benefits subsequently received.

NFT: non-fungible token—a cryptographic token which is not mutually interchangeable. Includes digital files such as art, audio, videos and other forms of creative work.

non-complying super fund: A super fund that is not residing in Australia or that has been issued with a notice of non-compliance because it does not comply with the *SIS Act 1993;* non-complying super funds do not receive the concessional tax rate and are taxed at 45 per cent.

non-resident: A person who does not normally reside in Australia and has no intention of living here; a non-resident is liable to pay tax only on income sourced in Australia. People who are temporarily in Australia for a working holiday are treated as non-residents for tax purposes, regardless of how long they are here.

notice of compliance: The ATO will issue this notice if it makes a determination that a fund complies with the *SIS Act 1993;* the determination is only made after an SMSF annual return has been lodged with the ATO.

objection: A formal challenge against an ATO assessment or decision.

option: An option is a form of right: if you receive an option, you make an agreement with the provider of the option, allowing you to buy shares or stapled securities during a certain time period, for a particular price (the exercise price); you then have the right, but not the obligation, to exercise the option.

PAF: private ancillary fund — a type of charitable trust typically created by family groups to undertake private philanthropy by pooling private donations and distributing them over time to chosen charities.

paid parental leave: A government benefit paid to a parent of a newborn child to help care for the baby; the pay is for up to 24 weeks (rising to a minimum of 26 weeks from 1 July 2026) at the minimum wage plus super and is taxable.

partnership: Two or more people in business with a common view to making a profit.

PAYG (pay-as-you-go) withholding: The tax deducted from an employee's wages by an employer and remitted to the ATO.

PAYG withholding variation application: A form, which is virtually a mini tax return, that estimates your taxable income for the upcoming year to reduce the tax deducted from your pay packet.

pension age: The age used to determine eligibility for certain government benefits, including the age pension; the pension age is currently 67 increasing to 70 by 2035.

positive gearing: The opposite of negative gearing; it occurs when the net rental income from an investment property, after deducting other expenses, is greater than the interest on the borrowings.

preservation age: The minimum age at which a member can access their preserved benefits; a benefit may be paid earlier if the member has met a condition of release; the preservation age varies depending on when the member was born. Currently 60 years.

preserved benefits: The superannuation fund benefits that you can access when you reach your preservation age and retire.

private ruling: Written advice you receive from the ATO about how it would interpret the tax laws in respect of a specific issue you raise.

PSI: Personal services income—business income that is principally derived via the personal exertion of an individual and is subject to certain tests in order to be assessable in a company or trust.

put option: The right, not the obligation, to sell underlying shares at an agreed price on or before the expiry date; a form of insurance in a falling market.

quantity surveyor: A professional within the construction industry who is recognised by the ATO to have the appropriate construction costing skills to calculate the cost of items for the purposes of tax depreciation schedules.

reduced cost base: The cost base of a CGT asset minus certain expenditure that has been allowed as a tax deduction; used to calculate a capital loss.

registered tax agent: A person who is authorised to give you advice in respect of managing your tax affairs and can lodge a tax return on your behalf; the fee they charge for their services is ordinarily a tax-deductible expense.

reportable fringe benefits: The grossed-up taxable value of certain fringe benefits provided to you on your payment summary.

reportable superannuation contributions: The sum of any contributions that you make to your superannuation fund for which you can claim a deduction in the financial year under Subdivision 290-C of the *Income Tax Assessment Act 1997,* and the contributions your employer makes for you.

resident: A person who normally resides in Australia; taxed on their worldwide income at the marginal tax rates.

Restart wage subsidy: A program that pays employers up to $10 000 (GST inclusive) over 6 months who employ and retain eligible job seekers who are 50 years of age or older, and who have been unemployed and on income support for six months or more.

rights issue: The right to buy additional shares direct from the company at a specified price (usually below market price) on a specified future date; usually linked to the number of shares you hold.

salary sacrifice: A strategy where you ask your employer to put an additional amount of your pre-tax salary into super.

self-assessment: The tax system in Australia where the onus is on you to declare to the ATO the correct amount of income you derive each year and claim the correct amount of tax deductions.

sell contract note: The invoice you receive from a stockbroker at the time you sell your shares; it will summarise the details of the transaction and can be used to calculate a capital gain or capital loss for taxation purposes.

senior Australian: Anyone aged over 65.

senior and pensioner tax offset (SAPTO): An effective tax-free threshold for eligible senior Australians of $32 279 for singles and $28 974 each for couples.

SFSS: Student financial supplement scheme—a voluntary loan scheme to help tertiary students cover their expenses while studying.

SG: Superannuation guarantee—compulsory super contributions paid every quarter by employers at a minimum of 12 per cent of employees' ordinary time earnings.

shareholder: A person who owns shares in a company.

share investor: A person who invests in the sharemarket with the predominant purpose of deriving dividends and long-term capital growth.

share trader: A person who is carrying on a business trading in shares with the predominant purpose of making a profit.

sharing economy: A mode of consumption whereby goods and services are not owned by a single user, but rather only temporarily accessed by members of a network and underutilised assets are shared, either for free or for a fee. Also known as the access economy, peer-to-peer (P2P) economy, or collaborative economy it includes Uber, AirbnB, Camplify, Menulog, Airtasker, Fiverr and Freelancer.

SIS: *Superannuation Industry (Supervision) Act 1993.*

SMSF: Self managed superannuation fund, also known as DIY super; a super fund that you manage yourself.

sophisticated investor: An investor as defined under Corporations Law who has a gross income of at least $250 000 in each of the two preceding years; net assets over $2 500 000; and/or controls at least $10 million of gross assets.

statutory method: A method used to calculate FBT on company cars based on the total number of kilometres travelled and applying a statutory fraction of 20 per cent to the cost of the car provided.

STP: Single Touch Payroll — an employer obligation to send employee payroll information such as gross wages, superannuation and PAYG withheld for every standard pay run.

super co-contribution: If you make personal contributions to your super and are otherwise eligible, the Federal Government will help boost your account with a super co-contribution of up to $500 per financial year; the amount of the co-contribution will depend on your total income level (you can earn less than $62 488) and the amount of personal contributions you make.

superannuation fund: A fund set up to finance retirement; benefits normally cannot be accessed until you reach your preservation age and retire from the workforce.

tax: Something we all hate paying and love to try and minimise ... legally!

taxable income: The amount of income that's liable to tax; taxable income equals assessable income less allowable deductions.

tax-deferred scheme: Employee share schemes that allow you to defer paying tax; generally, you will pay tax on the discount you receive when you acquire ESS interests in the financial year in which you acquired them; however, in certain circumstances, you may defer paying the tax for a period of up to 15 years.

tax-free threshold: The lowest tax bracket ($18 200) at which an Australian resident pays no tax; non-residents (including those on working holidays in Australia) cannot claim the tax-free threshold.

tax man: The nickname affectionately given to the Commissioner of Taxation and/or the Australian Taxation Office in general.

tax offset: A tax credit or rebate that you can use to reduce the amount of tax payable on taxable income you derive.

tax refund: Something we all love to get from the tax man each year.

tax ruling: A public ruling issued by the ATO to explain and clarify how the Taxation Commissioner interprets tax legislation in respect of a specific issue.

tenants in common: A legal arrangement where two or more people share ownership rights in a property or parcel of land. Unlike joint tenancy, when a tenant in common dies, the property passes to that tenant's estate where they have the right to leave their share of the property to any beneficiary as a portion of their estate.

TFN: Tax file number—a unique number issued by the ATO to individuals and organisations to increase the efficiency in administering tax and other Federal Government systems.

TFN withholding: Tax withheld at the highest marginal rate (47 per cent) on unfranked dividends and bank interest if you have not quoted your TFN; taxpayers need to include the amounts withheld in their tax return in order to receive the credit in their assessment.

total net investment loss: The sum for the financial year of the amount by which the individual's:

- deductions from financial investments are greater than their income from those investments
- rental property deductions are greater than their rental property income.

trust: A legal obligation binding a person (the trustee) who has control over the investment assets (for instance, a share portfolio) for the benefit of beneficiaries.

trustee: The individual or entity that has the responsibility of ensuring that the trust or super fund is operated in accordance with its trust deed; trustees must also comply with relevant legislation and regulations.

TtR: Transition to retirement—strategy available to those aged over 60 to access up to 10 per cent of their super each year to supplement their income.

under a legal disability: A beneficiary of a trust, such as a minor, a bankrupt or an insane person, who is not in a legal position to deal with a trust distribution.

unfranked dividends: Dividends paid by an Australian resident company from profits that have not had Australian company tax paid on them.

warrant: An option issued that gives the holder the right, but not the obligation, to buy from the issuer or sell to the issuer underlying shares at an agreed price on or before the expiry date.

wash sale: Selling shares to predominantly make a capital loss and gain a tax benefit, then buying the shares back immediately.

working holiday maker: A backpacker temporarily visiting Australia under visa subclass 417 (working holiday) or 462 (work and holiday). Pays 15 per cent on the first $45 000 of income earned and normal resident tax rates thereafter.

BIBLIOGRAPHY

A New Tax System (Goods and Services Tax) Act 1999.

A New Tax System (Goods and Services Tax) Regulations 1999.

Arnold, BR, Bateman, H, Ferguson A and Raftery AM 2015, *The size, cost and asset allocation of Australian self-managed superannuation funds*, Centre for International Finance and Regulation, working paper.

Australian Bureau of Statistics 2025, 5206.0 Australian National Accounts: National Income, Expenditure and Product: Table 1.

Australian Prudential Regulation Authority 2025a, Monthly. Authorised Deposit-taking Institution Statistics—December 2024.

Australian Prudential Regulation Authority 2025b, Quarterly Superannuation Performance—December 2024.

Australian Securities Exchange 2023, ASX Australian Investor Study 2023.

Australian Securities Exchange 2025, Historical market statistics—December 2024.

Australian Taxation Office 2025, Self-managed super fund statistical report—December 2024.

Australian Taxation Office 2024, Commissioner of Taxation annual report 2023–24.

Australian Taxation Office 2024, Taxation statistics 2021–22.

Bevacqua, J, Marsden, S, Morgan, A, Morton, E, Devos, K and Verma, S 2024 *Australian Taxation*, 3rd edn, Wiley, Melbourne.

Bird, R, Foster, FD, Gray, J, Raftery, AM, Thorp, S and Yeung, D 2018, *Who starts a self-managed superannuation fund and why?* Australian Journal of Management, Vol 43, Issue 3, pp. 373–403.

Futurity Investment Group 2025, The cost of education in Australia.

Fringe Benefits Tax Assessment Act 1986.

Income Tax Assessment Act 1936.

Income Tax Assessment Act 1997.

Income Tax Assessment Regulations 1997.

Income Tax Regulations 1936.

Pinto, D and Sadiq, K 2024, *Fundamental Tax Legislation 2025*, 11th edn, Thomson Reuters (Professional) Australia, Sydney.

Raftery, AM 2014, The size, cost, asset allocation and audit attributes of Australian self-managed superannuation funds, thesis.

Sadiq, K, Black, C, Hanegbi, R, Jogarajan, S, Krever, R, Obst, W, Clements, J and Walpola, S 2024, *Principles of Taxation Law 2025*, 17th edn, Thomson Reuters (Professional) Australia, Sydney.

Swyftx 2024, 4th Annual Australian Digital Assets Survey.

Thorp, S, Bird, R, Foster, FD, Gray, J, Raftery, AM and Yeung, D 2020, *Experiences of current and former members of self-managed superannuation funds* Australian Journal of Management, Vol 46, Issue 2, pp. 304–325.

Wolters Kluwer 2025, *Australian GST Legislation with Overview*, 28th edn, Wolters Kluwer, Sydney.

Wolters Kluwer 2025, *Australian Master Tax Guide*, 76th edn, Wolters Kluwer, Sydney.

INDEX

For an explanation of technical terms refer to the Glossary on pages 277–293.

Printed and bound by CPI Group (UK) Ltd, Croydon, CR0 4YY

07/12/2025

14785975-0001